MORE ESSENTIAL THAN EVER

INALIENABLE RIGHTS SERIES

. . .

GEOFFREY STONE AND OXFORD UNIVERSITY PRESS GRATEFULLY ACKNOWLEDGE THE INTEREST AND SUPPORT OF THE FOLLOWING ORGANIZATIONS IN THE INALIENABLE RIGHTS SERIES: THE ALA THE CHICAGO HUMANITIES FESTIVAL THE AMERICAN BAR ASSOCIATION THE NATIONAL CONSTITUTION CENTER THE NATIONAL ARCHIVES

More Essential Than Ever

. . .

THE FOURTH AMENDMENT IN THE

TWENTY-FIRST CENTURY

Stephen J. Schulhofer

OXFORD
UNIVERSITY PRESS

OXFORD
UNIVERSITY PRESS

Oxford University Press is a department of the
University of Oxford. It furthers the University's objective
of excellence in research, scholarship, and education
by publishing worldwide.

Oxford   New York

Auckland   Cape Town   Dar es Salaam   Hong Kong   Karachi
Kuala Lumpur   Madrid   Melbourne   Mexico City   Nairobi
New Delhi   Shanghai   Taipei   Toronto

With offices in

Argentina   Austria   Brazil   Chile   Czech Republic   France   Greece
Guatemala   Hungary   Italy   Japan   Poland   Portugal   Singapore
South Korea   Switzerland   Thailand   Turkey   Ukraine   Vietnam

Oxford is a registered trademark of Oxford University Press
in the UK and certain other countries.

Published in the United States of America by
Oxford University Press
198 Madison Avenue, New York, NY 10016

© Oxford University Press 2012

Library of Congress Cataloging-in-Publication Data
Schulhofer, Stephen J.
More essential than ever : the Fourth Amendment in the
twenty-first century / by Stephen J. Schulhofer.
p.   cm.
Includes bibliographical references and index.
ISBN 978-0-19-539212-8 (hardback)
1. United States. Constitution. 4th Amendment
2. Privacy, Right of—United States.
3. Searches and seizures—United States
4. Exclusionary rule (Evidence)—United States   I. Title.
KF9630.S38 2012   345.73'0522—dc23   2011047120

1 3 5 7 9 8 6 4 2

Printed in the United States of America
on acid-free paper

Contents

. . .

CONTENTS

Editor's Note

. . .

We hold these truths to be self-evident, that all men are created
equal, that they are endowed by their Creator with certain unalien-
able Rights....

—THE DECLARATION OF INDEPENDENCE

. . .

The Fourth Amendment is as clear as can be: "The right of the
people to be secure in their persons, houses, papers, and effects
against unreasonable searches and seizures, shall not be violated."
As is often the case in law, however, what seems clear is not. What
is a "search"? Is it a "search" for the government to track an individual's movements using a GPS? Is it a "seizure" for a police
officer to stop a person on the street to ask her questions? Is it a
"seizure" for a police officer to use a parabolic microphone to overhear a conversation two people have on a park bench? Is a conversation a "person, house, paper, [or] effect"? And when is a search
or seizure "unreasonable"? Is it "unreasonable" for government to

require all railroad engineers or political candidates to submit to random urinalysis tests? Is it "unreasonable" for government to require high school students to submit to such tests? And what is the appropriate remedy for a violation of the Fourth Amendment? Is it a civil action for damages by the person subject to the unreasonable search or seizure? Will that remedy effectively deter violations of the Fourth Amendment? If not, what other remedies might be appropriate?

In *More Essential Than Ever: The Fourth Amendment in the Twenty-first Century*, Professor Stephen Schulhofer explores these and other fundamental questions. Addressing the Fourth Amendment from both a historical and contemporary perspective, Schulhofer attempts to make sense of these questions in a constantly changing world.

Those who call for a narrow understanding of the Fourth Amendment often make two arguments: (1) Innocent people have nothing to hide; (2) The cost of the Fourth Amendment—hampering law enforcement—is too great. Schulhofer addresses these arguments in a thoughtful and illuminating manner. He unpacks the broader purposes of the Fourth Amendment, explores the dangers of unrestrained government authority to search and seize, and examines the ways in which the perceived trade-off between privacy and security can be misleading.

Another central question in the jurisprudence of the Fourth Amendment concerns the problem of constitutional interpretation in the light of changed circumstances. To what extent should the meaning or the application of the Fourth Amendment change in response to new technology, the emergence of well-armed professional police forces unknown in the eighteenth century, or simply new patterns of social life that have emerged in contemporary urban society. Modern technology, for example, enables government to learn more about the daily lives and decisions of Americans than ever before in our history. How do these changes play into the proper interpretation of the Fourth Amendment? Originalists might argue that the meaning of the Fourth Amendment was fixed at the time it was drafted. If technology has changed the playing field, then it is not for courts to bring the Fourth Amendment up to date. In 1790, for example, the Framers understood a "search" as a physical intrusion into a physical place. What, then, of government interception of phone and email conversations? In *More Essential Than Ever*, Professor Schulhofer considers how different approaches to constitutional interpretation play out in the realm of the Fourth Amendment, where the implications of originalism are especially stark.

Another important dimension of Fourth Amendment jurisprudence turns on changes in the makeup and disposition of the Supreme Court over time. The task of defining "unreasonableness" necessarily requires judges to balance competing values. Schulhofer clearly notes and discusses those instances in which a Court that has generally become more "conservative" over the past five decades has allowed the particular values of individual justices to determine the meaning and scope of the Fourth Amendment. Whether this is good or bad is, of course, open to debate, but as Professor Schulhofer demonstrates in *More Essential Than Ever* the Court's increasingly narrow interpretation of the Fourth Amendment in an era of expanding government surveillance raises serious questions about our constitutional future.

Geoffrey R. Stone, November 2011

Acknowledgments

...

This book is the outgrowth of many years of teaching and writing about the Fourth Amendment. Over that time a great many colleagues and students have helped me to clarify my thinking and to better understand the many puzzles of law and policy that swirl around the Fourth Amendment. I am especially grateful to Geoffrey Stone for the invitation to contribute to this series, for countless constructive conversations and suggestions, and for the insight and rigor that he brought to his probing, line-by-line critique of the manuscript. For helpful comments on various drafts, I owe thanks as well to David McBride, the editor-in-chief for Social Sciences at Oxford University Press, and to my colleagues Albert Alschuler, Barry Friedman, Erin Murphy, Katherine Strandburg, and Tom Tyler. Greg Anrig, the Vice President for Policy and Programs at the Century Foundation, has been instrumental in helping me bring Fourth Amendment concerns to bear on national security policy. For resourceful research assistance, I thank Danielle Byam, Rachel Dizard, Andrea Lofgren, Julie Mecca, Lauren Pedley, Elliot Siegel, and David Tracy. Finally, but first in every important sense, I am grateful beyond measure to my wife, Laurie Wohl, for her unfailingly generous support and selfless forbearance.

MORE ESSENTIAL THAN EVER

CHAPTER ONE

. . .

Introduction

The right of the people to be secure in their persons, houses, papers, and effects, against unreasonable searches and seizures, shall not be violated, and no Warrants shall issue, but upon probable cause, supported by Oath or affirmation, and particularly describing the place to be searched, and the persons or things to be seized.

—THE FOURTH AMENDMENT (1791)

. . .

ABUSIVE SEARCHES—ransacking of homes, rummaging through papers and effects—figured prominently among the grievances of the American colonists and became potent causes of the American Revolution. That history gave birth to the Fourth Amendment. Its prohibition of "unreasonable searches and seizures" was once considered a cornerstone of American liberty.

Yet social and technological transformations of the past fifty years, reinforced most recently by the powerful information-gathering capacity of computers and the Internet, now cast a large cloud over the Fourth Amendment. For some, Fourth Amendment safeguards have become especially important, a crucial shield against the staggering surveillance capabilities available to the government. For others, the notion that we can shield information about ourselves is naïve, if not obsolete. The relevance and meaning of the Fourth Amendment seem increasingly obscure.

The usual formula proclaims that government conducts a prohibited "search" when it unjustifiably intrudes on a "reasonable expectation of privacy." But what, in the modern world, can "privacy" really mean? Against the background of electronic data collection that now enters nearly every corner of modern life, how much privacy can we expect? And given the distinctive dangers of the modern world, themselves fueled by powerful new technologies, can a preference for privacy over public safety still be considered "reasonable"?

In the aftermath of the September 11 attacks, the administration of George W. Bush sought expanded authority for surveillance, and Congress obliged by granting counterterrorism officials robust new legal tools for intercepting electronic communications. The Patriot Act also gave the administration a broad array of new powers for investigation and surveillance through old-fashioned, nonelectronic techniques, including secret "sneak-and-peek" searches of homes and secret access to medical and financial records, library borrowing histories, and many other previously private records and documents. Despite opposition to these measures from traditional civil liberties quarters and from the newly influential community of techies and bloggers, public resistance to these powers is increasingly scattered and ambivalent.

One reason has been *fear*, especially fear that the next terrorist strike could cause fatalities on a scale that would dwarf the events of 9/11. Many citizens are convinced that it is best to give up certain liberties in order to minimize the risk of a potentially catastrophic attack. In the common cliché, there is a supposed trade-off between civil liberties and national security: increase liberty and the nation is inevitably less safe; to enhance security, we must sacrifice liberty. And the liberty most quickly marked for sacrifice is privacy. Judge Richard Posner, for example, insists that "in an era of global terrorism and...weapons of mass destruction, the government has a compelling need to gather, pool, sift, and search vast quantities of information, much of it personal."[1]

The willingness to surrender privacy is reinforced by doubts about whether many traditional sorts of privacy remain important. Simple fatalism also plays a role. Because encroachments on privacy seem so widespread and inexorable, many Americans believe that almost everything about their lives is already "out there." Others are convinced that any small shards of privacy still remaining will not last much longer and are scarcely worth fighting for.

Going further, many now question whether there *should* be any right to keep our phone calls and email messages private. Because Internet browsing and on-line shopping already expose much of our lives to commercial data banks, in ways over which we have almost no control, why should government officials charged with our safety be the only ones denied access to that information? The late Harvard law professor William Stuntz wrote that in the face of social disorder and transnational threats, continuing support for privacy is a "disease" that undermines public safety and national security.[2] For some scholars, privacy has practical importance only when it shields disreputable facts. Therefore, they say, informational privacy is simply not a value we ought to protect. The common refrain is "Why should I worry about government surveillance? I have nothing to hide." The Fourth Amendment, on this view, is now antiquated and potentially dangerous.

Despite the prevalence of such attitudes, privacy retains an intuitive, if poorly understood, appeal. The unnerving theme of *1984*— "Big Brother Is Watching You"—has lost none of its ominous and demoralizing power. The twenty-first-century Fourth Amendment is thus caught between incompatible instincts: an all-seeing Big Brother is antithetical to a free society, but most efforts to restrain the government's appetite for information seem both risky and futile.

In this book, I hope to sort out these competing ideas. By examining the historical roots of the Fourth Amendment and the ways it continues to benefit us, I hope to explain why it is important and why maintaining the vigor of its safeguards is more essential than ever. I will also explore how we can do this despite accelerating technological changes that often seem beyond our capacity to control.

A good way to start is to identify four recurring myths that fuel skepticism about the Fourth Amendment. It is common to assume that Fourth Amendment privacy is primarily or exclusively concerned with *information*. Conventional wisdom also holds that private information means *secret* information, that most of this privacy is *already gone*, and that privacy (or whatever remains of it) is about *concealing misconduct*.

These widely accepted notions do have a kernel of truth—but no more than that. Each of these ideas is mostly a distortion, in essence a myth. And these myths prevent us from seeing the true core of the Fourth Amendment. For the amendment offers a guarantee not merely of secrecy but of *personal autonomy*. It offers a shelter from governmental intrusions that unjustifiably disturb our peace of mind and our capacity to thrive as independent citizens in a vibrant democratic society.

PRIVACY: SECRECY VERSUS AUTONOMY

Consider first the idea that privacy means shielding information. Everyone understands the principle that the Fourth Amendment should prevent government officials from rummaging through your private diary without good reason. But this natural idea easily leads to the dangerous notion that the Fourth Amendment therefore should not protect anything you willingly reveal to others. It was this notion that led a federal appeals court, in an opinion by Judge Richard Posner, to hold that the Fourth Amendment does not require a sheriff to obtain a warrant before seizing and towing away a person's mobile home. As long as the sheriff did not go inside, Judge Posner reasoned, the officer did not see anything that was not already exposed to the public.

This is far too narrow a view, and the Supreme Court rightly (and unanimously) rejected it.[3] As the Court recognized, the Fourth Amendment protects us from unjustified government actions that disturb our peace and tranquility, not only from those that interfere with secrecy. The language of the amendment is explicit on this point, affirming "the right of the people to be *secure* in their persons, houses, papers and effects."

Those who equate privacy with secrecy need some other term to describe our desire for a buffer against government interference with our security. Others find it natural to include that need in what they consider their "privacy," just as we could say that the police would disturb our privacy if they used a loud sound truck to blast routine announcements late at night. But regardless of labels, the Fourth Amendment (which does not use the term "privacy") undoubtedly protects this interest in not having our peace of mind disrupted by unreasonable government intrusion. The same principle explains why an arrest without probable cause violates the Fourth Amendment, regardless of whether any "secret" information is exposed. These intrusions on security and tranquility—in short, on our autonomy—violate the Constitution, even when they do not expose our secrets.

INFORMATIONAL PRIVACY: SECRECY VERSUS CONTROL

The idea that privacy means secrecy is too narrow even when we think only about personal information, like the contents of a journal. Suppose I give you my diary and urge you to read it. No one would think you are violating my privacy when you do so. The reason is that privacy is not about the information itself, no matter how personal it may be. Instead, this aspect of privacy—informational privacy—is about my *right to control* what others see, and in this example I have given you my permission. Although the diary is no longer completely secret, it remains private, in the sense that I (and others whom I trust) still have the right to control who can see it.

Privacy typically has little to do with information we conceal from the whole world. Rather, what makes privacy valuable are the relationships and projects we develop by sharing information with others. Even when we have no desire to keep our ideas completely secret, we attach great importance to ensuring that we and our associates remain able to determine when and how those ideas are disclosed to others. Our relationships and the thoughts we exchange within them are private.

For these reasons, there can be no doubt that informational privacy is about *control*, not about secrecy. But as later chapters explain, Supreme Court decisions have created great confusion about this crucial point. If the government listens in on a conversation between you and a friend, without having probable cause or a warrant, the intrusion clearly violates the Fourth Amendment, even though you have chosen to "expose" your thoughts by revealing them to another person.[4] Likewise, if the government searches your hotel room without probable cause or a warrant, the intrusion violates the Fourth Amendment, even though you allowed the hotel's cleaning staff to enter the room and see the same things only a few minutes before.[5] But if you transmit a telephone number to your telecom provider so that it can connect your call, the Supreme Court permits the government to intercept the transmission and record the number you dialed, even without probable cause. In this situation, the Court said, "a person has no legitimate expectation of privacy in information he voluntarily turns over to third parties."[6] And the Court likewise held that your Fourth Amendment protections disappear even when the information you share is highly personal—as with financial information you share with your bank.[7]

The Court's occasional (though inconsistent) willingness to equate privacy with complete secrecy now assumes enormous significance, because modern life so often requires us to convey information to health care professionals, Internet service providers, financial institutions, and the like. A central concern of this book is to demonstrate the importance for all Americans of preserving our capacity to limit the government's access to facts about ourselves— even when practical necessities or goals we choose to pursue oblige us to share those facts with trusted individuals and institutions for limited purposes. Like autonomy and security, *control* over personal information plays an essential role in enabling citizens to achieve independence and individual fulfillment.

THE ALLEGED DISAPPEARANCE OF PRIVACY

A related myth is that privacy, or at least informational privacy, is already gone. The common assumption is that technological change and global economic pressures have reduced privacy to an attractive but now obsolete ideal. Many look back on the nineteenth and twentieth centuries as simpler times that, however appealing, are irretrievably lost. They believe that for practical purposes most of our privacy has long since slipped away and that we will soon lose the little that remains, regardless of what we may wish or what the law may say.

This attitude is plausible only if privacy means complete secrecy. On that view of the matter, we have indeed lost much of our privacy. But if it makes sense to equate privacy with complete secrecy, the erosion of privacy is nothing new. Long before computers and the Internet, even before Alexander Graham Bell invented the telephone, Americans revealed intimate details of their lives to others, in conversations with their doctors, lawyers, and bankers, in correspondence with lovers and colleagues, in meetings to plan crimes or simply to organize business ventures or political protests. These Americans had no desire to live in a world of complete secrecy. But it would not have occurred to them that by entering into relationships with others, they had given *the government* unrestricted access to any information they revealed to trusted social and professional associates. The Founding Fathers who met in taverns to plot the Revolution certainly understood the privacy of shared information. No one in those days thought that these relationships made the idea of privacy meaningless or that the exchange of confidential information would allow the government to conduct unrestricted searches against the will of the participants.

Once we understand that the essence of privacy is not secrecy but the right to control—the right to decide what gets revealed to whom and for what purposes—we can see that nothing in modern life makes the loss of privacy inevitable. Even on Facebook, you get to decide who can be your "friend." If you choose friends who are indiscreet, they may betray your confidence, but that fact need not give government the power *to force* the disclosure of everything you share, without meeting Fourth Amendment requirements.

Of course, not all social processes can be tamed by human will. But this one can be, if we wish to do so. In later chapters, I argue that we can (and must) assert our right to control the information we share with others and that it is more important than ever for the Fourth Amendment to protect that right vigorously, as it traditionally did.

NOTHING TO HIDE?

Much of the skepticism about privacy flows from the feeling that legally enforceable privacy—a set of rules to block investigation by the government—impairs our welfare far more than it benefits us. The pervasive assumption seems to be that those who most insistently claim a right to privacy are usually seeking to conceal some sort of misconduct. As a practical matter, therefore, the Fourth Amendment seems only to protect criminals or to shield information that is at best disreputable. Few themes are more common in debates about privacy than the constant refrain that relaxation of Fourth Amendment safeguards should give no cause for concern because good citizens have "nothing to hide."

This is another notion that is plausible, influential, and profoundly mistaken. Informational privacy is not only about shielding misconduct or embarrassing facts. How many of those who have "nothing to hide" would volunteer to send their coworkers and next-door neighbors a copy of all—*all*—of their email? How would you feel if every conversation you've had in the past year had been secretly recorded and posted on the Internet? We can hardly doubt that this prospect would inhibit perfectly lawful conversations and relationships.

Even when our thoughts and actions are innocuous, we may not want others to know every detail. Some people may even prefer not to appear as conventional as they really are; they may seek to maintain a bit of mystery. Privacy—understood as our ability to preserve a sheltered space, to control when we reveal information about ourselves and to whom—is indispensable for the capacity to feel at peace, to try out new ideas, to think and grow as an independent individual.

Government officials who insist that law-abiding citizens should feel no need for privacy are the first to demand privacy for their own papers and discussions, claiming that unconstrained reflection and well-considered decisions would be impossible without it. Indeed, when our Constitution was drafted, the Framers deliberated under tight security and insisted that the progress of their work remain confidential. For the same reason, we go to great lengths to prevent eavesdropping on discussions in the jury room; the overriding importance of ensuring privacy for those deliberations is obvious to all.

Many who claim to have "nothing to hide" probably understand these points well. Whether they realize it or not, they likely feel a need for privacy many times each day as they go about their perfectly innocent routines. No one wants to live her life in a fish bowl. When privacy skeptics say they have nothing to hide, what they no doubt mean is only that they do not fear the limited exposure that might result if some of their personal information was occasionally seen by government investigators, whose jobs require them to stay focused on ferreting out signs of serious criminality.

The privacy skeptic's real objection, then, is not that law-abiding citizens never need confidentiality, but only that they should not worry about keeping details of their private lives from police and prosecutors whose only interest is to catch those who are up to no good.

This tendency to accept surveillance for law enforcement purposes overlooks one of privacy law's most important objectives. This goal is less familiar than the well-understood desire for closed doors and shades on our windows, but it lies at the heart of our Fourth Amendment. When we think of privacy as a constitutional principle, we must remember that the well-being it aims to foster is not only personal but *political*. In seeking to protect the autonomy of each citizen, the Fourth Amendment supports our ability to flourish as individuals, but it also serves, perhaps more importantly, to sustain the foundations of a truly *democratic* society. We naturally associate democracy with the right to vote, but political freedom requires many other constitutional safeguards. In fact, democratic objectives pervade our Bill of Rights. Democracy is not simply a matter of majority rule, because a legitimate government and a healthy society must permit political disagreement and protect minorities of all sorts—whether they be defined by race, ethnicity, religion, politics, culture, sexual orientation, or other characteristics that distance them from the mainstream. Modern human rights conventions are now explicit in embracing this conception: in the name of securing "a democratic society" (not merely a *majoritarian* society), they limit the ability of elected legislatures to interfere with many core liberties of the individual.[8]

No less than freedom of speech or the press, protection from unwarranted government surveillance ranks among these core liberties that are essential to democracy. Indeed, as a precondition for well-developed political expression and association, privacy is intimately connected to freedom of speech. Government spying may not worry the average citizen who reads best-selling books, practices a widely accepted religion and adheres to middle-of-the-road political views. But no one doubts that surveillance can have an inhibiting effect on those who are different, chilling their freedom to read what they choose, to say what they think, and to join with others who are like-minded. As we shall see in the next chapter, the Fourth Amendment grew out of bitter experience in the suppression of political dissent. It was designed to assure outsiders some breathing room by creating a buffer between them and the power of the state. Human rights conventions applicable throughout the world endorse the same principle, insisting that safeguards for privacy and personal security are indispensable prerequisites for individual freedom and democratic government.*

Any law-abiding citizen who feels in any way out of step with the social or political establishment readily understands this need for a buffer—for protection against unrestricted government scrutiny. But those who place themselves squarely in the mainstream benefit personally as well. The great majority of Americans want to live in a vibrant, diverse society where a wide range of views can be expressed, where new ideas can be explored. Nearly every American, even the most conventional, wants to live in a democracy, after all. So all of us need the Fourth Amendment: When unrestricted search and surveillance powers chill speech and religion, inhibit gossip, and dampen creativity, they undermine politics and impoverish social life for everyone.

The catch here is that we don't want the sheltered space for nonconformity and political disagreement to become a sheltered space for planning crime. And the Fourth Amendment would have just that effect if it left police and prosecutors with no capacity to search in private areas. Antipathy to the Fourth Amendment is almost always based on the assumption that it works in exactly that way. If it did, serious qualms would indeed be in order.

But the Fourth Amendment does no such thing. The genius of the amendment is that it does not ban all invasions of privacy; it

---

* For example, the Universal Declaration of Human Rights (1948) guarantees the right to "security of person" (art. 3) and prohibits "arbitrary interference with [any person's] privacy, family life, home or correspondence" (art. 12). The International Covenant on Civil and Political Rights (1966) contains virtually identical guarantees (arts. 9, 17), as does the European Convention on Human Rights (1950) (arts. 5, 8). In the case of the European Convention, moreover, these guarantees are judicially enforceable.

merely regulates them to ensure that searches will be well justified, tightly focused efforts, not casual fishing expeditions. In fact, the Fourth Amendment expressly *authorizes* invasions of privacy, permitting investigators to intrude on the most intimate areas of our homes, papers, and effects when they can show probable cause and obtain prior judicial approval in the form of a narrowly drawn search warrant. Because its goal is to promote personal security, not unqualified privacy, the amendment does not eliminate certain government powers but only seeks to build confidence that they will be properly used. Its means to that end is not an inflexible prohibition but only a requirement of *accountability*. It provides a buffer, not a wall.

Ironically, therefore, the individuals the Fourth Amendment seeks to safeguard are not criminals but the very people who have "nothing to hide." It protects the privacy rights of the innocent, but it does not preclude police from invading the privacy of those who are reasonably suspected of committing or planning crimes. Through its requirement of accountability, it gives legitimacy to essential law enforcement powers and aims to ensure that they are not used so loosely that they needlessly intrude on law-abiding citizens. In this respect, as in the others just mentioned, an effective Fourth Amendment fosters the sense of personal security that is necessary for individual autonomy and political liberty in a free society.

SETTING BOUNDARIES

These are the ideas that this book seeks to develop and illuminate, considering their application in both traditional searches and in technologically sophisticated forms of surveillance. Across a wide range of situations, the mandate of the Fourth Amendment collides with other perceived social needs. The specific issues discussed in subsequent chapters will enable us to examine in concrete terms the costs of too much privacy and the appropriate ways to limit Fourth Amendment claims. Robust government powers of investigation are as important as ever. But sound responses to contemporary crime and terrorism do not require us to abandon the Fourth Amendment—far from it. A close look at modern intelligence gathering and law enforcement will make clear the kinds of surveillance powers and safeguards that are necessary in an increasingly complicated and dangerous world.

Chapter 2 examines our Fourth Amendment tradition, discussing its four-hundred-year history and the early landmark cases, in England and the colonies, that shaped our understanding of government powers and individual rights. The colonists deeply resented the Crown's efforts to search private homes at will. They insisted that a magistrate approve every search in advance, by finding specific reasons to suspect the particular homeowner in question. The commitment to warrants was not a blind attachment to an ancient ritual. It reflected a deeply felt determination to constrain discretion and ensure accountability whenever officials conducted searches and seizures.

Chapter 3 brings the discussion up to date by focusing on the problems we face in contemporary law enforcement. Does the requirement of prior judicial approval that was so important to the American colonists still make sense today when police need to search a house for drugs that can be hidden or destroyed in an instant? Does the warrant requirement make sense when police need to arrest a felon who can easily disappear into the anonymity of a vast modern city? Should police have to obtain a warrant before searching the private areas of vehicles that can quickly move out of the jurisdiction?

Few of these issues, if any, could have been in the minds of those who framed our Bill of Rights. Many people believe that when problems are new, the Constitution doesn't speak, and that deference to "original intent" leaves elected officials and the police free to craft solutions unconstrained by the Fourth Amendment. Throughout this book, therefore, an unavoidable concern will be that of determining the legitimate approach to constitutional interpretation. Chapter 3 demonstrates that respect for constitutional text and the intentions of the Framers cannot always require inflexible application of the rules that the Framers themselves considered "reasonable." Because the effect of those rules is often so different in our world than it was in theirs, faithful adherence to their intentions requires an *adaptive* originalism. Indeed, we shall see that despite occasional claims to the contrary, *all* the justices of the Supreme Court accept and apply this flexible approach, tailoring old common-law rules to present conditions, so that our Fourth Amendment continues to further the goals that the Framers themselves sought to realize.

If specific contemporary problems were not in the minds of the Framers, the importance of personal security and autonomy, the dangers of discretion, and the need to ensure accountability certainly were. Nothing in modern developments makes traditional insistence on oversight and accountability obsolete. If anything, the truth is just the reverse: social and technological change since the eighteenth century—the emergence of professional police, the advances that enable them to carry small but deadly firearms, and their access to increasingly powerful surveillance tools—all make accountability even more important. Chapter 3 discusses the safeguards necessary to maintain our traditional respect for privacy in an ever-changing world.

Chapter 4 turns to policing on the streets. Contrary to the impression fostered by *Law and Order* and other TV dramas, modern police spend little of their time solving major crimes, searching for evidence, or catching perpetrators in hiding. Instead, their principal assignment is simply to maintain order on sidewalks, roads, and highways—a task that is much less glamorous but equally difficult and important. To do their jobs, they often need to question individuals, conduct pat downs, or inspect backpacks and packages. What limits (if any) does the Fourth Amendment impose on this sort of routine patrol activity? Would the Fourth Amendment's Framers see broad police powers as a "reasonable" response to modern urban life, with its dangers and disorder? Or would they see police control over freedom of movement in public spaces as similar to the searches and arrests that preoccupied Americans in the eighteenth century?

Particularly difficult problems arise when police base their suspicions on "profiles." Should this tactic ever be allowed? If so, what factors can be considered—youth? shabby clothing? religion? ethnicity? What would the Framers make of *racial* profiling? The challenge is to give police needed efficacy and flexibility without abandoning our commitment to equality and evenhanded law enforcement. Chapter 4 examines these issues.

Chapter 5 turns to means of social regulation that increasingly eclipse traditional methods of law enforcement. Over time, government's missions have grown, and specialized enforcement agencies have proliferated. In an effort to enhance public safety, our homes, cars, and luggage are now routinely targeted for scrutiny, often by officials other than the police, and often without any reason to suspect us of criminal behavior. Even our bodies are subjected to suspicionless inspection, through urinalysis drug testing, airport body scanners, and the like.

Strict adherence to traditional Fourth Amendment requirements (probable cause and a warrant) would pose difficult problems for personnel attempting to screen airline passengers or for fire marshals and city building inspectors attempting to ensure compliance with construction safety codes. In the name of practicality or "reasonableness," the Supreme Court has relaxed the warrant and probable

INTRODUCTION

cause requirements when a search serves special needs distinct from ordinary law enforcement. Although this approach affords flexibility, the notion of "special needs" is infinitely elastic. Does it mean that citizens can be routinely subjected to highway roadblocks, home inspections, and urinalysis drug testing whenever "public health and safety" is invoked as a justification? Chapter 5 examines this growing threat to our privacy and spotlights the importance of preserving accountability and judicial oversight, even when these searches are considered merely "administrative."

Chapter 6 considers the issues posed by "new" methods of search and surveillance. Some—like wiretapping and electronic eavesdropping—are now more than a half century old. For decades, the Supreme Court held that these surveillance techniques were beyond the reach of the Fourth Amendment because they did not involve a *physical* entry into any private place. By the 1960s, however, advances in technology and growing appreciation of its dangers had made that view increasingly untenable. The Court finally recognized that electronic invasions of privacy can be just as intrusive as physical ones.[9]

That step solved one set of problems but created a host of new ones. A search typically lasts a few minutes or at most a few hours. Can a wiretap that "searches" for weeks or months ever be "reasonable"? How can a warrant "particularly describe" the items that the wiretap is permitted to seize? If placement of a wiretap or hidden microphone requires a warrant, do police need a warrant to use other sense-enhancing devices—a high-resolution camera? thermal imaging equipment? a flashlight? Which investigative tools are too powerful to be deployed without oversight?

Chapter 6 also examines a more recent technological transformation—the revolution in accessing, aggregating, and analyzing information. A great deal of intensely personal information is now reduced to digital form; it can be endlessly duplicated, at virtually

[19]

no cost, distributed to an almost limitless audience of people unknown to us, and then used for purposes that are likewise limitless and unknown. Chapter 6 shows how these developments, in combination with the Supreme Court's artificial "third-party" disclosure doctrine, threaten the privacy, autonomy, and personal security that are necessary to sustain individual freedom and political democracy. Chapter 6 also shows how traditional Fourth Amendment concerns can be respected in a landscape that renders privacy vulnerable from so many new directions.

Chapter 7 takes up the contentious problem of national security. The lethal combination of smaller, cheaper weapons of mass destruction and increasingly simple means of delivering them has created in contemporary America a perception of never-ending danger—a danger of devastation on a scale the Framers could not have imagined.

Throughout our history, the government has claimed the right to conduct searches and surveillance without judicial approval when national security is involved. But in the 1970s, Congress sought to rein in these previously unrestricted powers. The Foreign Intelligence Surveillance Act of 1978 (FISA) acknowledged the government's need for flexibility and secrecy in this domain but created a system of oversight to prevent abuse. After 2001, however, Congress and the executive branch took many steps to weaken the FISA regime. Chapter 7 examines the complexities of FISA and the ways that the Patriot Act, along with other post-9/11 developments, have afforded the executive branch ever-greater latitude in the use of national security powers.

Most people, academics and ordinary citizens alike, assume that in order to make the nation less vulnerable, we must grant greater powers to the executive and sacrifice many traditional forms of privacy. As we will see in Chapter 7, however, liberty and national security are not always in conflict. Indeed, measures that weaken accountability and oversight—the Fourth Amendment's central mechanisms—often *undermine* public safety, leaving us *more* exposed to attack.

A concluding chapter brings together the broad array of settings in which Fourth Amendment concerns arise. In the course of this book, we will have confronted SWAT teams that break into a private home to search for drugs, patrol officers who stop minority teenagers who look "out of place" in a wealthy neighborhood, school principals who require athletes to submit to random urine tests, and FBI agents who conduct surveillance of journalists and Muslim religious leaders. The threats to privacy have changed enormously over the centuries. But the importance of privacy to the well-being of individuals and to the flourishing of democracy has not diminished in the least. Fourth Amendment safeguards that have been honed for centuries—warrants, constraints on discretion, oversight, and accountability—have become, if anything, increasingly necessary. Far from being obsolete, they are more essential than ever in the high-tech world of the twenty-first century.

· · ·

CHAPTER TWO

Our Fourth Amendment Tradition

The poorest man may, in his cottage, bid defiance to all the forces of the Crown. It may be frail; its roof may shake; the wind may blow through it; the storm may enter; the rain may enter; but the King of England may not enter; all his force dares not cross the threshold of the ruined tenement.

—WILLIAM PITT, SPEECH ON THE EXCISE BILL,
HOUSE OF COMMONS (MARCH 1763)

· · ·

THE RIGHT TO A PROTECTED private space—the famous principle that "a man's house is his castle"—long predates the English common law. Respect for privacy is evident not only in biblical and Roman sources but even in preliterate societies and, for that matter, even in the animal kingdom. Biologists have noticed that primates and many other mammals seek periods of solitude or intimacy within a small group. More than a thousand years before Pitt's stirring declaration in the House of Commons, the Roman statesman

Cicero declared: "What is more inviolable...than the house of a citizen?...This place of refuge is so sacred to all men, that to be dragged from thence is unlawful."[1]

But just as respect for privacy is universal, so too is government's appetite for information. Culture and historical experience shape each society's conception of the government powers its citizens will tolerate and the specific safeguards they demand.

Conflict between the king and his subjects over the right to privacy reached a fever pitch, both in the colonies and in Britain, in the mid-eighteenth century. Our core ideas about the limits of official authority were formed in the crucible of that controversy. At a time when this experience was still fresh, the proposals that became our Fourth Amendment were brought forward and adopted. And the timing was no mere coincidence. The American Revolution itself was in no small measure a product of impassioned struggles over search and seizure that came to a head in the 1760s.

According to a long common-law tradition, a *general* warrant—one that authorized officials to apprehend anyone they suspected of a crime, or to search any place they suspected might contain stolen goods—was void. The person executing it could be resisted or sued for trespass to person or property. Although the history leaves some details obscure, the main principles emerge clearly, and to this day they continue to shape our views about safeguards against government intrusion. Three points were repeatedly emphasized in the formative eighteenth century period—judicial authorization, specificity, and the control of executive discretion. The officer attempting a forcible entry into a private dwelling was required to have a warrant issued by a judge, not by an executive official; the warrant had to describe its target with particularity; and it could not leave much discretion to the officer charged with executing it.

Chief Justice Matthew Hale's treatise, written in the late 1600s, summarized the common-law view. Valid warrants, Hale said, must be "judicial acts," identifying the specific person to be arrested or the specific place to be searched, and they could be issued only after the judge had independently considered the grounds for suspicion and found "probable cause." A general warrant, he added, was "not justifiable, for it makes the party [executing it] to be in effect the judge."[2]

Alongside this understanding, however, it became common for a high officer of the king's administration, the secretary of state, to enforce libel laws and collect revenue through various assistants to whom he issued *general* search and arrest warrants on his own authority. These warrants went largely unchallenged for decades, so that in actual practice the law governing search warrants appeared to be in flux. Then, in the 1750s and 1760s, onerous new revenue measures brought the issue to the fore and gave it great importance.

ENGLAND IN THE MID-EIGHTEENTH CENTURY

John Wilkes, a member of Parliament in the 1760s, was the kind of figure that has become familiar in contemporary American politics, a tireless critic and ardent tax protester who made himself a constant thorn in the government's side. One of his complaints targeted the new Cider Tax, which applied to homemade products that tax collectors might find in almost any household. Even in the House of Lords, the tax had evoked strong protest because "subjects, who from the growth of their own orchards, make Cyder and Perry [fermented pear juice], are subjected to the most grievous mode of excise; whereby private houses of peers, gentlemen, freeholders, and farmers are made liable to be searched at pleasure."[3]

Stepping up his criticisms, Wilkes began to publish anonymous pamphlets denouncing the government. One of these, entitled *The North Briton, No. 45*, was a sarcastic attack on a speech in which the king had expressed support for the Cider Act. In 1763, no longer willing to tolerate Wilkes's defiance, Lord Halifax, the secretary of state, issued a warrant ordering four king's messengers "to make strict & diligent search for the Authors, Printers & Publishers of a seditious and treasonable paper entitled, The North Briton Number 45, ... [and] to apprehend & seize [them], together with their papers."[4]

The messengers were indeed diligent. They arrested forty-nine individuals, some in their beds, and often on the flimsiest justification. Dryden Leach, a printer, was seized in the middle of the night, together with all his papers, on the basis of nothing more than the fact that one of the messengers "had been told by a gentleman, who had been told by another gentleman, that Leach's people printed the paper in question."[5] Eventually, the messengers located the man who had printed *The North Briton, No. 45*, and learned that its author was Wilkes. They proceeded to arrest him, searched all his desk drawers, and seized all of his papers, including even his will.

Wilkes was imprisoned for the offense of seditious libel. But meanwhile, he and the others swept up in the searches brought suit against the messengers. At the first trial, involving one of the printers, Chief Justice John Pratt emphatically condemned the Halifax warrant as illegal: "To enter a man's house by virtue of a nameless warrant, in order to procure evidence, is worse than the Spanish Inquisition; a law under which no Englishman would wish to live an hour."[6] The damage award—£300—was extraordinary, more than two years' income for a printer at the time. Pratt acknowledged that a much smaller figure—£20—normally would have sufficed in light of "the small injury done to the plaintiff [and] the inconsiderableness of his station and rank in life." But he ruled that the jury's reaction nonetheless was justified: "they saw a magistrate over all the king's subjects, exercising arbitrary power, violating Magna Carta, and attempting to destroy the liberty of the kingdom...; they heard the King's Counsel...endeavor to support and maintain the legality of the warrant in a tyrannical and severe manner. These are the ideas which struck the jury...and I think they have done right in giving exemplary damages."[7]

The £300 verdict was only the beginning. Other printers recovered damages of £200–£300 each, and Leach was awarded £400. Wilkes won verdicts of £1,000 against Halifax's undersecretary and an astonishing £4,000 against Halifax himself. Overall, the authorities incurred expenses totaling £100,000. Meanwhile, Chief Justice Pratt did nothing to appease the government. In indignant language soon to become famous, he gave his full support to the jury, heartily approving its remarkable damage award for Wilkes: "The defendants claimed a right [to seize] papers, upon a general warrant,...where no offenders' names are specified in the warrant, and therefore a discretionary power given to messengers to search wherever their suspicions may chance to fall. If such a power is truly invested in a secretary of state,...it certainly may affect the person and property of every man in the kingdom, and is totally subversive of the liberty of the subject..., a rod of iron for the chastisement of the people of Great Britain."[8]

Wilkes and Pratt immediately became popular heroes in England. News of the cases soon spread to America, and Wilkes maintained a lively correspondence with key figures in the colonies, including Samuel Adams, John Adams, and John Hancock.

Another English case of the period concerned a much narrower warrant. In 1762, Halifax issued a warrant to find and arrest one John Entick, the author of an allegedly seditious tract. The warrant named Entick specifically but did not identify the particular items to seized; to the contrary it instructed the messengers to take away all of Entick's books and papers. With respect to the seizures, therefore, their mandate amounted to a "general" warrant, which the messengers executed with enthusiasm. In a suit against the messengers, the jury awarded Entick £300.

Again the court upheld the verdict, issuing an opinion that our Supreme Court hailed many years later[9] as a Fourth Amendment landmark. The English court first rejected the government's argument that the secretary of state's peacekeeping functions in effect made him a "justice of the peace," an official who had authority to issue search warrants. That conclusion, in the years immediately preceding the adoption of our Bill of Rights, became crucial in determining what a "warrant" is—an authorization from a court, not one issued by an executive officer. The warrant's function, of course, is to *control* the executive, to impose accountability; it can hardly serve its purpose if the executive is permitted to oversee itself.

Another feature of Entick's case resonates with particular force today—the court's focus on the intrusion into the privacy of *information*, an injury that was distinct from the invasion of Entick's house, his arrest, and the physical seizure of his property. In upholding the jury's generous damage award, the court emphasized that the sweeping confiscation of the papers had inflicted a unique harm. If the law permitted such seizures, the court said, "it would destroy all the comforts of society; for papers are often the dearest property a man can have. [They] are so far from enduring a seizure, that they will hardly bear an inspection; and though the eye cannot by the laws of England be guilty of a trespass, yet where private papers are removed and carried away, the secret nature of those goods will be an aggravation of the trespass, and demand more considerable damages."[10]

TROUBLE IN THE COLONIES

The Entick and Wilkes episodes were of great interest across the Atlantic because they arose just when the colonies were embroiled in their own struggles with the Crown. Until 1760, there had been relatively few major tensions between the colonists and their British rulers. But in that year, the government began for the first time to make a determined effort to enforce laws that imposed stiff import taxes and barred trade with French possessions in the Caribbean. The key tool of enforcement was the "writ of assistance"—a type of general warrant issued to customs officers by the colonial court.

The name is revealing. The law enforcement officials of that time and their deputies were a far cry from today's heavily equipped SWAT teams that surround suspected stash houses and break down doors in search of drugs and other contraband. In their ability to bring force to bear, colonial constables and customs agents cannot even be compared to the ordinary contemporary traffic cop. Instead, the eighteenth-century customs agent was armed with little more than his writ. He depended on the homeowner's cooperation and, absent that, on the help of other citizens. His writ commanded all bystanders to render assistance, and those who failed to do so could be held in contempt of court.

Though issued by a judge, the writ of assistance was even broader than Halifax's general warrants, because it was not directed toward the investigation of any particular crime. It permitted the chief customs officer and his deputies to search anywhere, on suspicion of any offense. It called for no "return" (the report and inventory of seizures that must be filed with the court after executing an ordinary search warrant), and it remained in effect almost indefinitely. However, in October 1760, about the same time that the British government resolved to ramp up its enforcement of the trade restrictions, George II died, and the governing statute provided that all writs of assistance would expire six months after the king's death. As a result, just when the customs laws were about to become a flashpoint, new writs had to be authorized, and this development set the stage for a test of royal power in the Superior Court of colonial Massachusetts.

Sixty-three Boston merchants filed a petition against the issuance of new writs of assistance. They insisted that by the basic principles of British liberty, a court could legally grant only "special writs, directed to special officers, and to search certain houses, especially set forth in the writ,...upon oath...that [the applicant] suspects such goods to be concealed in THOSE VERY PLACES HE DESIRES TO SEARCH."[11]

The merchants retained James Otis, Jr., one of the colony's most prominent attorneys, to represent them. In a packed courtroom, Otis startled and energized the observers by launching an incendiary attack not only on general writs but on the broad abuses of British power they had allowed. The writ of assistance, he maintained, "places the liberty of every man in the hands of every petty officer...; everyone with this writ may be a tyrant. [Because] there's no return, a man [executing such a writ] is accountable to no person for his doings [and may] spread terror and desolation around him. [N]ot only deputies but even THEIR MENIAL SERVANTS ARE ALLOWED TO LORD IT OVER US."[12] The writs, Otis declared, were "monsters in the law" and "instruments of slavery...and villainy,...a kind of power, the exercise of which in former periods of English history, cost one King of England his head."*[13]

Otis and the merchants lost their argument, at least in the short term. The *Wilkes* and *Entick* cases had not yet been decided in England, and without those rulings as a guide, a compliant Massachusetts court under Chief Justice Thomas Hutchinson ruled in

---

* Otis evidently was referring to the execution of Charles I in 1649, following his conviction for high treason. Since oppressive searches and seizures had not figured prominently in the accusations against Charles, Otis apparently sought to suggest an analogy between the abuses of his own time and the tyrannical powers Charles had claimed—notably his attempts to rule and levy taxes without parliamentary consent.

favor of the government. At the end of 1761, Hutchison issued a new writ of assistance to Charles Paxton, the chief customs officer of the Port of Boston.

But the seeds of resistance had been planted. John Adams, then a fledgling lawyer in his twenties, later described the reaction in the courtroom: "Mr. Otis's oration against the Writs of Assistance breathed into this nation the breath of life.... Every man of a crowded audience appeared to me to go away, as I did, ready to take arms against Writs of Assistance. Then and there was the first scene of opposition to the arbitrary claims of Great Britain. Then and there the child of Independence was born."[14]

The rest is a well-known story. In the other colonies, judges began to refuse applications for these writs. In Massachusetts, popular opposition soon made them impossible to enforce, especially after passage of the Stamp Act in 1765. Rioters protesting the stamp tax destroyed the home of Hutchinson, the chief justice who had ruled against Otis, and in Falmouth, townspeople gave the required "assistance" by forcibly retaking the seized goods and restoring them to their owner. After the growing rebellion culminated in the Declaration of Independence in 1776, many of the colonies, having claimed sovereignty, wrote search-and-seizure safeguards into their own founding documents. Ratification of the federal constitution in 1789 was quickly followed by adoption of the Bill of Rights. Drawing on the state search-and-seizure restrictions, the first Congress framed and endorsed the present language of the Fourth Amendment, which is set forth at the outset of chapter 1.

THE LEGACY OF REVOLUTION

The history leaves no doubt on several key points. The nation's Founding Fathers and the others who drafted and ratified the Fourth

Amendment detested unrestricted government searches of the home. They were determined to outlaw the general warrants that had authorized those intrusions. In their eyes, a valid warrant for search or seizure could be issued only by a judge, on the basis of specific grounds for suspicion, and it would have to target a particular individual for arrest or a specific place to be searched for specific things.

Against that background, however, the Framers gave the Fourth Amendment a peculiar structure (peculiar, at least, to modern eyes and ears), because taken literally, the amendment neglects to prohibit the one practice that the Framers were most uniformly and intensely concerned about. The problem arises because the amendment has two distinct clauses that do not easily fit together. The second clause ("no Warrants shall issue, but upon probable cause") ensures that warrants must be drafted with particularity. But nothing in the amendment expressly forbids searches conducted *without* a warrant; the first clause bans only "unreasonable" (not "warrantless") searches and seizures. As a result, the amendment imposes stringent requirements, spelled out in detail, whenever a warrant is used, but it provides no explicit rule for determining when a warrant is necessary. And when a warrant is unnecessary, the amendment imposes only a "reasonableness" requirement, with no concrete limitations at all.

Although the words of the Fourth Amendment were chosen with care, and we can be quite certain about the abuses that gave rise to them, the provision as written poses several puzzles. Does it permit warrantless searches even in private homes, limited only by a loose requirement of reasonableness, or does it implicitly require a warrant for searches within a domicile? Does it implicitly require a warrant to search in other locations as well? What exactly did the Framers have in mind?

From today's perspective, it seems absurd to think that those who opposed abusive searches would impose strict requirements for obtaining a warrant but permit law enforcement officers to escape those requirements whenever they chose not to get a warrant at all. Would the English courts have decided the *Entick* and *Wilkes* cases differently if Lord Halifax's messengers had conducted their searches and seizures without using any warrants whatsoever? That seems hard to imagine.

One way to make sense of the Fourth Amendment is to assume that any search of a dwelling without a valid warrant would be unreasonable on that ground alone. Given its history, the amendment *must* implicitly disfavor warrantless searches of the home. The first clause of the amendment would then be understood as prohibiting searches and seizures in a dwelling place without a valid, narrowly drawn warrant, except when a particular situation makes it unusually difficult to obtain one. For the past half century, that reading has largely prevailed in the Supreme Court, though (as we shall see in later chapters) the Court has often divided in deciding what circumstances make it unreasonable to expect police to seek a warrant.

One challenge to the prevailing view comes from Akhil Amar, who argues that the reasonableness requirement—not the warrant requirement—is the real heart of the Fourth Amendment.[15] The explanation, Amar claims, is that a valid warrant would give the officer conducting the search a complete defense in any suit for damages. A warrant with that effect should be extremely difficult to obtain. On Amar's view, then, the Framers would prefer *warrantless* searches, because the officer acting without a warrant would owe damages for an unreasonable search and would therefore have a strong incentive to proceed carefully.

The historical record, however, does not support this subtle argument. At the time, poorly armed constables and king's messengers had difficulty enough in attempting to execute a search even when they held a warrant and the right to command the assistance of bystanders. Under the circumstances, the likely eighteenth-century alternative to a search pursuant to a warrant was not a warrantless search but no search at all. It is hard to imagine that the Framers, with their antipathy toward the overbearing officials who sought to enter their homes, would have disfavored searches guided by warrants if the alternative had been what it would be today—the prospect of searches by heavily armed police squads permitted to intrude without prior judicial approval.

Extensive research, most notably by Thomas Davies, confirms that the Framers had no desire to encourage warrantless searches and feared only those warrants that failed to confine the scope of the intrusion. There is no indication that Amar's concern about preserving the threat of damage awards was ever expressed at the time. In contrast, the Framers did express, clearly and emphatically, their view that narrowly drawn warrants were a vital means of protection.[16] Otis himself had extolled the ancient pedigree and practical value of warrants—so long as the officer's mandate was targeted specifically to "THOSE VERY PLACES HE DESIRES TO SEARCH."[17]

One key to the Framers' preference for specific warrants is that the traditional warrant process requires a "return" to the issuing court and therefore ensures immediate oversight of the manner in which the search has been executed. Another is that the requirement of a warrant prevents improper searches *before* they happen, so that the targets of government suspicion need not rely on trespass litigation to obtain redress after the fact. James Otis stressed exactly this point, asking whether, after a house has been illegally searched, "is it enough to say, that damages may be recover'd...? Are we *perpetually* to be expos'd to outrages of this kind, & to be told for our *only* consolation, that we must be *perpetually* seeking to the courts of law for redress?"[18] In both ways, the warrant process was the mechanism for assuring the king's subjects that royal powers were being exercised under judicial oversight and within the bounds of the law.

CONSTRAINING DISCRETION

Perhaps the single most important feature explaining the preference for specific warrants is that they confine the discretion of the officer conducting the search. Today, many Americans assume that debates about the value and dangers of police discretion are a uniquely contemporary preoccupation. In our lifetimes, racial and ethnic prejudice, overt discrimination, and police-community tensions in America's inner cities have made us especially aware of the potential abuses of discretion. Many believe that modern social conditions require special sensitivity to these dangers. Others, including some current members of the Supreme Court, see anxiety about discretion and worries about racially biased policing as products of a distinctive episode in our history; they argue that these concerns have been rendered obsolete by progress in race relations. But resistance to discretion did not begin in the 1960s, and it has never been grounded solely in concerns about race. Awareness of the need to limit law enforcement discretion has been a prominent part of our Fourth Amendment tradition from the start.

Interestingly, modern concerns about discretion are not identical to those that dominated in the eighteenth century. Now, we associate harmful discretion with the mistreatment of minorities, the poor, and other disadvantaged groups. In earlier centuries, the primary fear was more or less the reverse: men of property found it offensive that mere messengers and assistants could enter their homes and search through their effects at will. In Entick's case, for example, when the secretary of state claimed a statutory power to issue warrants to his messengers, Entick's counsel responded that "a messenger...is nothing more than a mere porter, and Lord Halifax's footmen might as well be said to be officers within the statute."[19] Otis, writing in block letters, objected that "MENIAL SERVANTS ARE ALLOWED TO LORD IT OVER US."[20] James Madison, when arguing for a constitutional ban on general warrants, emphasized the need to constrain Congress's legislative power; he feared that popular majorities would enact legislation authorizing broad warrants, to the disadvantage of the new nation's propertied elite. But whether the concern centers on victims who are wealthy or poor, there is no doubt that resistance to discretion lay at the heart of the traditional objection to general warrants.

It is important to emphasize the ancient roots of this concern, because so much of recent Fourth Amendment discussion suffers from historical amnesia, treating mistrust of the police as a peculiarly contemporary fixation, as if it were rooted solely in experiences peculiar to the United States since our Civil War. That view is totally at odds with the historical record of opposition to law enforcement discretion.

Chief Justice Hale, for example, writing in the seventeenth century, explained that a general warrant was void because it "makes the party [executing it] to be in effect the judge."[21] The leading English treatise of the early eighteenth century said the reason for prohibiting general warrants was that "it would be extremely hard to leave it to the Discretion of a common Officer to arrest what Persons, and search what Houses he thinks fit."[22] In 1763, Chief Justice Pratt, upholding the damages awarded to Wilkes, deplored the general warrant as a "discretionary power given to messengers to search wherever their suspicions may chance to fall."[23] Two years later, in a case brought by the printer Dryden Leach, Lord Mansfield denounced the Halifax warrant on the ground that "it is not fit, that the...judging of the information [said to justify the search] should be left to the discretion of the officer. The magistrate ought to judge; and should give certain directions to the officer."[24] In 1769, Blackstone, whose *Commentaries* were the colonists' most important source of authority on English law, relied on these cases to explain that the decisive flaw in general warrants was their delegation to enforcement officers of decisions that should be made by a judge.[25] In the 1770s and 1780s, just before the framing of the Bill of Rights, judges in Pennsylvania, South Carolina, and Virginia condemned general warrants in language that expressly objected to the "discretion" they conferred on subordinate officers.[26]

In short, the preference for warrants grows out of concerns that have been central to our thinking about searches and seizures since at least the eighteenth century. The foundational commitment was to shield the autonomy of the individual by affording some insulation against the intrusive powers of government. And that commitment required procedural mechanisms that would achieve four specific goals—to constrain law enforcement discretion; to provide an independent judicial gatekeeper; to prevent improper searches at their inception; and to ensure accountability by requiring a "return" to the court, so that damage suits after the fact did not become the only means for discouraging abuse.

SEARCHES AND SEIZURES OUTSIDE THE HOME

Although the colonial protests focused primarily on the special sanctity of the home, many searches and seizures occurred elsewhere. Ships were detained, warehouses were searched, and wagons were inspected. Fleeing offenders were arrested in village streets and taverns. Compared to the controversial searches of private houses, we have less evidence about actual practices in these other areas, and those practices (whatever they were) did not trigger the intense debates that surrounded searches of homes under writs of assistance. The lack of controversy may suggest that eighteenth-century practice in these matters was acceptable to those who adopted our Fourth Amendment, or it may suggest only that no one had made it a priority to challenge them. But the common law had developed rules to govern some of these issues, and these are therefore an important part of our traditional understanding of searches and seizures.

Under the common law, a constable could make a warrantless arrest for any offense committed in his presence. He also could make a warrantless arrest for an offense committed outside his presence, but only if the offense was a felony and the officer had "reasonable cause" to believe that the person arrested had committed it. Absent these circumstances, the constable could arrest only under the authority of a warrant—a specific, judicially issued warrant like those required for the search of a home. A private citizen could make an arrest under the same circumstances. In fact, the law conferred no special powers on peace officers; if an improper arrest prompted the alleged offender to sue, the defenses available to the constable were identical to those available to any other citizen.

The law governing searches was less well defined. Ships were frequently seized and inspected without a warrant; wagons and other property were occasionally searched without a warrant as well. But our information about the applicable law is slender. The most common type of search outside the home was the search of an alleged offender at the time of arrest. These searches appear to have been routine, but again, the available legal authorities are thin and sometimes ambiguous; the exact extent of the power to search incident to arrest is subject to debate. The ambiguity results in part from the fact that such searches were much less important at that time than they became later. Forensic evidence was of course unheard of, and eyewitness testimony was the principal form of proof. As a practical matter, the power to search individuals was seldom of consequence, except in connection with the seizure of untaxed goods and the recovery of stolen property.

Against that background, it seems clear that when arrests and searches satisfied well-settled common-law requirements, they were considered reasonable and therefore permissible under the Fourth Amendment. And although the common-law rules could be quite technical, it seems equally clear that a failure to satisfy them would make a search "unreasonable" and therefore unconstitutional. We cannot be entirely sure about the originally intended meaning of reasonableness. But the best historical evidence indicates that for those who spoke out against abusive searches, and especially for John Adams, who inserted the word into the draft language that became the Fourth Amendment, "unreasonable" meant "against reason" or "inherently illegal at common law."[27]

These common-law rules, together with the colonial struggles over searches and seizures, have passed on to us a rich tradition of respect for personal security and informational privacy. They also help us in a more concrete way, by identifying specific safeguards and procedures to protect the "right of the people to be secure in their persons, houses, papers, and effects." Yet that history lies far in the past. Today, some members of the Supreme Court, Justices Scalia and Thomas in particular, insist that the history must continue to control our understanding of what the Fourth Amendment requires. But others question how much weight (if any) the eighteenth-century practices should have for us in the twenty-first century.

THE DISTANT WORLD OF COLONIAL AMERICA

Breathtaking technological change provides an obvious reason for these doubts. Eavesdropping was common in 1789, and there is no reason to think that the Framers viewed it as a violation of the Fourth Amendment. They recognized that prying eyes and ears could invade precious aspects of privacy (as happened when the messengers rummaged through Entick's papers), but for them, "searches and seizures" implied a *physical* trespass.

Yet technological advances have enormously enhanced the eavesdropper's ability to disturb our security, while reducing almost to zero our capacity to exclude him. There is now a widespread consensus that the Framers' larger purpose—to safeguard our right to be secure—requires us to discard the notion that the Fourth Amendment regulates only physical intrusions. But having agreed to eliminate that boundary, we remain unsure of how to replace it with other principles that will respect the Fourth Amendment's essential but limited mission.

Another profound change is less often discussed but much older and even more perplexing in its implications. That transformation can be summed up in one word—urbanization. Although the point is simple, its ramifications are multidimensional.

Within only a few decades after 1789, the size and density of America's cities exploded. A flood of immigration obliterated whatever homogeneity and social cohesion the towns had previously enjoyed. Crime and disorder assumed far more troubling proportions. Mechanisms of social control that had proved adequate for centuries—a constable, a night watchman, and the community "hue and cry"—suddenly became pitifully insufficient. By the 1840s, society began for the first time to make plans for full-time police forces. In their size, organization, armament, training, and mission, they had little in common with the instruments of law enforcement known to the Framers. Powers of search and seizure became vastly more important for maintaining social order, but in the hands of professional police, they acquired vastly greater potential for abuse.

In the eighteenth century, most counties of any size had a full-time sheriff charged with looking after the local jail and summoning juries, but it was not his job to patrol the streets. That function fell to ordinary members of the community, who took time away from their regular jobs to serve a turn without pay, and without a weapon or uniform, as the constable (a daytime assignment) or as the watchman at night. The constable was expected to keep an eye on the streets while performing a variety of other civic functions—for example, monitoring the slaughterhouses. The duties of the night watch included maintaining the street lamps and announcing the time every hour. Neither the constable nor the night watchman had any responsibility for investigating crimes, and if they happened to confront a perpetrator, they were seldom effective against one who chose to run away or resist.

To apprehend a fleeing felon, the constable's principal weapon was the "hue and cry," calling on citizens to join in giving chase. The only other option, when a larger force was required, would be for the sheriff to summon a *posse comitatus* (literally "the power of the county"), which again was a group of volunteers from the public at large. (The Latin term passed into common parlance as the "posse" that plays a dramatic role in so many movies about the old West.) Colonial records show constant complaints about the performance of the constables and night watchmen—not (as we might expect today) for being overly aggressive but for being too passive and ineffectual. Often they literally slept through their assigned turn on the job.

Eighteenth-century law enforcement was thus a small, poorly organized, amateur affair, a far cry from the sizeable force of well-armed, full-time police who only a few years later become a constant presence on the streets of American cities and towns. The Framers almost certainly assumed that the common-law framework they knew was adequate to serve their twin goals of providing for public safety and individual privacy. But just as the citizens of the eighteenth century did not anticipate parabolic microphones or the Internet, they did not foresee social changes that began to revolutionize law enforcement only a generation later. The shift from amateurs to professionals, and all that went with it, peace officers on the street much greater ability to deploy force to protect the community and also much greater ability to threaten the rights of those who might attract their disfavor.

The Framers thus left to subsequent generations the difficult but inescapable task of preserving our Fourth Amendment tradition under constantly evolving circumstances. Respect for their intentions—what many label "originalism"—is the obligation of every conscientious judge, but that respect cannot take the form of an unreflective commitment to old rules that now have radically different effects in practice. As we shall see, genuine respect for the Framers must involve an *adaptive originalism*, tied not to original rules but to original principles. Specific eighteenth-century doctrines give us guidance, but often they must be tailored to new social conditions, if they are to sustain the values that the Framers held essential to the well-being of a democratic society.

· · ·

CHAPTER THREE

Searches and Arrests

Fourth Amendment freedoms...are not mere second-class rights but belong in the catalog of indispensable freedoms. Among deprivations of rights, none is so effective in cowing a population, crushing the spirit of the individual and putting terror in every heart. Uncontrolled search and seizure is one of the first and most effective weapons in the arsenal of every arbitrary government. [T]he human personality deteriorates and dignity and self-reliance disappear where homes, persons and possessions are subject at any hour to unheralded search and seizure.

—JUSTICE ROBERT H. JACKSON (1949)

· · ·

WE NOW JUMP roughly two hundred years forward, to consider the Fourth Amendment as it applies in the modern world. We will leave for later chapters the most novel and technologically sophisticated developments—the reach of electronic surveillance, the implications of the Internet, and the threat of weapons of mass destruction.

Instead, this chapter focuses on more routine social problems (violence, greed, drunk driving, addictive drugs) and the ways that government seeks to address them with the aid of conventional searches and arrests.

Because our subject is constitutional rights, we cannot ignore general issues that command attention across all topics in constitutional law. What, for example, is the importance of the precise language used in the constitutional text? Does a provision's wording or the "original intent" of its Framers always control?

Much of the public takes it as obvious that these criteria—text and original intent—are the only appropriate considerations. Indeed, at our judicial confirmation hearings, senators typically maintain that no other basis for constitutional decision can possibly be legitimate. As "originalists," they insist that the constitution, properly understood, can forbid only those specific practices that the Framers themselves intended to condemn. Yet very few judges and Supreme Court justices are "originalists" in this sense. Inevitably, they pay attention to a wide range of considerations, and they have no doubt that they are justified in doing so. In practice, our Constitution is unquestionably a living, evolving document.

This reality is not just a recent development. The historical evidence makes clear that the Framers themselves were not "originalists" in the narrow, literal sense. For most matters addressed in the Bill of Rights, they did not want to bind judges to eighteenth-century practices; they themselves intended to create a "living constitution." From the start, therefore, the Fourth Amendment represented much more than a code of specific law enforcement procedures. It was an expression of foundational values and a mandate to the courts to safeguard those values in the face of changing circumstances. Eighteenth-century practices are a starting point, but they cannot be the end of the matter.

Consistent with that view, one best described as *adaptive originalism*, the Supreme Court has rarely treated historical details as conclusive. Whether the Court's governing majorities have been "liberal" or "conservative," the justices have almost always agreed that Fourth Amendment interpretation must take into account the impact of police practices in the modern world. They have disagreed strongly, however, about the continuing importance of the Fourth Amendment's traditional commitment to judicial checks on law enforcement discretion. And contrary to conventional wisdom, it is the current Court, with its "conservative" majority, that has been most ready to set aside traditional Fourth Amendment requirements.

Although the Court's criminal procedure decisions are notoriously complex, several clear patterns emerge. The Court continues to insist on strong justification and prior judicial approval for police intrusions into private dwellings; a person's home is still her castle. But for matters outside the home, most of today's justices have repeatedly abandoned the fundamental value judgment originally embodied in the Fourth Amendment: an appreciation of the need to afford each citizen the security of a buffer against intrusive governmental powers. And likewise these justices have paid less and less heed to the structural mechanism the Framers saw as essential to achieve that end: the system of independent judicial oversight that ensures a place for appropriate law enforcement needs while also preserving personal privacy, individual dignity and political freedom. As Justice Lewis Powell explained in a 1972 opinion for the Court: "The historical judgment, which the Fourth Amendment accepts, is that unreviewed executive discretion may yield too readily to pressures to obtain incriminating evidence and overlook potential invasions of privacy and protected speech."[1] But in the contemporary Court, a majority of the justices has increasingly put police convenience above these original Fourth Amendment priorities.

SEARCHING THE HOME

Today, as in the eighteenth century, the search of a home requires a judicially issued warrant. The warrant must be based on the judge's finding of probable cause to believe that specific evidence or a specific criminal offender will be found at a place that is described with particularity. Before the police enter, they must "knock and announce," identifying themselves and stating their purpose. And they must give the homeowner a reasonable opportunity to open the door and admit them. Yet modern law enforcement presents situations that seem to require exceptions.

Take the "knock-and-announce" requirement. Police may receive information indicating that a drug ring keeps its stash at a particular apartment. If a judge finds probable cause and issues a warrant, the police are then entitled to search the apartment for drugs. But do they have to knock and announce their purpose? If so, the drug dealers are sure to make the drugs disappear (flushing them down the toilet, for example) before admitting the officers. A strict knock-and-announce requirement would defeat the purpose of the search. Even worse, by alerting the occupants, the police would give the dealers an opportunity to draw their weapons and prepare to shoot it out on their own terms. Here the knock-and-announce tradition finds itself in conflict with modern law enforcement realities. The Supreme Court therefore allows the police to retain the element of surprise. In cases like these, magistrates can issue a "no-knock" warrant, and officers are then permitted to break down the door and burst in without warning. The Framers may or may not have contemplated this exception to the ancient knock-and-announce requirement, but it is surely a reasonable adjustment to the problems posed by modern firearms and readily destructible evidence.

To remain faithful to the spirit of necessity that justifies this exception, however, no-knock searches must be confined to limited circumstances. Prosecutors have urged the Supreme Court to permit entry without warning in all felony drug cases, because dealers typically are armed and the evidence is almost always easy to destroy. This view is at once understandable and deeply troublesome. The overriding principle is the sanctity of the home, with its distinct importance as a refuge for privacy and security. Although no-knock searches can serve a valuable law enforcement purpose, they are also uniquely unsettling, even terrifying, for the homeowner, who of course may ultimately be innocent of any wrongdoing.

Most drug busts featured on TV crime dramas show a big-time dealer caught in a hideout where piles of heroin or cocaine are found. In real life as well, illegal searches often produce evidence of criminality—those are the searches we hear about when a guilty offender objects to them in court. It is easy to forget that illegal searches are often fruitless, and their victims are often law-abiding members of the community. "Probable cause" requires only a *probability*, not a certainty of wrongdoing; suspicions, even when justified, often prove to be mistaken. The innocent are therefore at risk even when a search is perfectly legal. Restraint and judicial oversight remain extremely important even when the police believe in good faith that probable cause exists.

In May 2003, New York City police, acting on an erroneous tip, burst into the home of Alberta Spruill, using a flash grenade to enhance the element of surprise; she suffered a fatal heart attack as a result. In 2006, police acting on an informant's tip executed a no-knock warrant and entered the Atlanta home of Kathryn Johnston, who grabbed her gun and was shot and killed by the officers; the informant later confessed that he had made up the address under pressure to give information to the police. In December 1999, a

Denver SWAT team executing a no-knock warrant stormed into the home of Ismael Mena, a husband and father of nine, and shot him to death when he reached for a gun; after the shooting, the police discovered that they had entered the wrong address. Numerous similar incidents are reported across the country. In one, Cory Maye, an innocent homeowner asleep in his bed, suspected a burglary and opened fire, killing a police officer; Maye was sentenced to life imprisonment for the homicide.

Recognizing the threat that unannounced entry poses to a long-standing Fourth Amendment priority—security in the home—the Supreme Court unanimously held in 1997 that no-knock searches are permissible only when there are specific grounds to believe that a prior warning will expose officers to danger or cause evidence to be destroyed.[2] But in its most recent decisions, the Court has treated the knock-and-announce requirement—one of the oldest known to the common law—as a mere technicality and has refused to exclude evidence that police gain by disregarding it.[3]

The no-knock entry is troublesome because it makes the search especially stressful and alarming. Another modern technique—the so-called sneak-and-peek search—poses the opposite problem. The homeowner can be lulled into a false sense of security when police conduct their search secretly, with no notice at all.

In a traditional search, officers present the occupant with a copy of the warrant when they enter and give her an inventory of all items taken when they leave. Her ability to observe the search and see exactly what is seized provides a valuable safeguard against abuse. Sometimes, however, the occupant's presence at the time of the search can prevent the police from accomplishing their objective.

Again, the modern business of illegal drugs illustrates the problem. Agents investigating a suspected lab for "cooking" methamphetamines may want to observe the lab secretly, in order to identify its suppliers without alerting them that they are under suspicion. Or when agents have a warrant authorizing them to place a listening device in an apartment, they obviously cannot tell the owner what they are doing. Strict adherence to the traditional notice rules would defeat the purpose of these searches. The capacity to enter and search secretly is now increasingly important because investigations of terrorism and organized crime often require the installation of secret surveillance tools.

In situations like these, judges have issued warrants that permit covert entry—a "sneak-and-peek" or, in more formal terms, a "delayed-notice" search. The occupant eventually receives the customary notification, but only a week or more afterward. As in the case of no-knock searches, the modern tactic of delayed notification is not at odds with Fourth Amendment values, provided that judges permit it only when the need is convincingly demonstrated. And the courts have generally followed this approach. Although the Supreme Court has never ruled on the constitutionality of covert entry and delayed-notice searches that are not needed to install bugging equipment,[4] appellate courts have upheld them when the reasons for secrecy and the length of time until notice is given are explained to the judge and approved as reasonable at the time the warrant is issued.

EXIGENT CIRCUMSTANCES

A more fundamental challenge to Fourth Amendment traditions arises when the police claim that special circumstances require them to enter a home without any judicial warrant at all. If officers chase a robbery suspect down an alley and see him go into a house at the end of the block, do they have to wait for a warrant before they can enter to arrest him? In these "hot pursuit" situations, the Supreme Court has held that prior judicial approval is impractical and therefore has allowed the police to enter without a warrant, provided they have probable cause to believe that an offender has just fled inside.[5]

Such "exigent" circumstances are not uncommon. As a result, the core prohibition against entering a home without prior judicial approval, however sacrosanct in theory, could quickly shrink in practice. Just three years after the Supreme Court's first "hot pursuit" ruling, a Louisiana case illustrated the dilemma. Police, having a warrant to arrest Donald Vale, set up surveillance outside his home. When a car drove up and the driver honked its horn, Vale came out of the house, had a brief conversation with the driver, went inside, and then came back out again. The driver took something from Vale and drove away. Police blocked the car and saw the driver attempt to hide the drugs that Vale presumably had just sold him from a stash kept somewhere in the house. The officers arrested Vale on his front steps. Knowing that Vale's mother and brother were inside, where they could easily destroy the drugs before police could return with a search warrant, the officers conducted the search right away and found narcotics in the rear bedroom.

Although Vale's family could have gotten rid of the drug stash quickly, the Supreme Court held that this imminent threat did not necessarily establish exigent circumstances. The problem, the Court said, was that the police had received information against Vale some time before setting up their surveillance and had even obtained a warrant for his arrest. Because it was unclear exactly what the police knew *prior* to their stakeout, the Court felt that prosecutors had failed to prove why they were unable to seek a warrant in advance for the search of the house. In other words, the need for immediate police action at the time of the arrest wasn't enough; "exigency" also requires the officers to prove that they had *no prior opportunity* to obtain a warrant before the need for immediate action arose.[6] Cases like this reaffirm the Court's strong commitment to the traditional requirement of prior judicial approval for intrusions into the home.

The Court has resisted warrantless searches of the home even when police *did not* have a prior opportunity to get a warrant. In a 1990 Minnesota case, police were looking for Rob Olson, the suspect in a robbery-murder at a local gas station. When a woman called police to report that Olson was staying in an apartment above hers and had just come home, police immediately surrounded the building and called on Olson to surrender. After he failed to come out, they stormed into the apartment, guns drawn, and found Olson hiding in a closet. Again, there was a need for immediate action, and this time the police could not have obtained a search warrant before rushing to the scene. But the Supreme Court nonetheless held the entry illegal.

The problem this time was that the officers could have prevented Olson's escape simply by maintaining their stakeout and waiting to enter the apartment until a search warrant had been issued. *Some* immediate police action was necessary, but the Court held that *entering* the apartment was not, because the police could have accomplished their purpose in a less intrusive way.[7] The fact that police personnel would be tied up in the stakeout makes the *Olson* decision even more telling. Inconvenience for law enforcement, the Court held, could not take priority over the citizen's protection against warrantless intrusion. True exigency exists only when there is a need for immediate action, no prior opportunity to get a warrant, *and* no less intrusive alternative.

In all these ways, the Court has largely remained faithful to our original Fourth Amendment tradition when the privacy of a domicile is at stake. The Court has insisted on probable cause and judicial approval *prior* to the intrusion whenever possible, and it imposes demanding requirements for police to qualify for any exception to this rule. The Court has emphasized the need for judicial oversight and strong checks on law enforcement discretion. Unfortunately (and inexplicably), the Court has followed a very different approach when police intrusions affect well-recognized privacy interests outside the home.

ARRESTS

Although the Fourth Amendment speaks in equal terms of the right to be secure in our houses and our persons, the eighteenth-century common law permitted constables to make a warrantless arrest for any crime committed in their presence. In addition, they were authorized to arrest without a warrant for *felonies* not committed in their presence—provided that the suspect was found in a public place and the constable had reasonable grounds to believe that the suspect was in fact the perpetrator. This rule was well settled at the time of the Framing, and the first Congress endorsed it in a 1792 statute authorizing federal marshals to make warrantless felony arrests. The difficulty is that this felony-arrest rule, though clear enough in the eighteenth century, has no straightforward meaning in modern circumstances.

Its ambiguities became apparent in a case involving stolen credit cards. Federal agents had probable cause to believe that Henry Watson had committed the offense, and they had ample time to get a warrant. Instead, they located Watson at a restaurant and made the arrest without a warrant. Theft of the cards and credit card fraud are classified as felonies. But would the common law have permitted a warrantless arrest for these offenses in 1792? The fact that credit cards were unknown is not in itself the problem, because we can easily imagine similar sorts of misconduct that did exist at the time. The difficulty is that in 1792 a roughly comparable crime would have been a misdemeanor. In addition, the modern offense of credit card fraud carries a penalty (imprisonment) that was associated with misdemeanors in 1792; at that time all felonies were punishable by death. So it is not clear whether Watson's theft-like offense is a true "felony," as that term was understood in the eighteenth century.

Similar puzzles arise for thousands of other modern crimes. Many of them simply did not exist in the eighteenth century. Others, though familiar at the time, were considered misdemeanors. How, then, does the common-law requirement, presumably reflected in the Fourth Amendment, apply today? It became necessary for the Supreme Court to resolve an issue the Framers never confronted—what the common-law rule actually was. Did it permit a warrantless arrest only when the crime was punishable by death? Only when the crime was extremely serious? Or did it allow an arrest without a warrant for any offense that carried the "felony" label?

Given the traditional Fourth Amendment commitment to prior judicial approval, it seems natural to assume that the exception for felony arrests should be interpreted narrowly, just as the Court has done when considering the exigency exception for searches of a domicile. If anything, it would seem that the safeguards surrounding an arrest should be stronger than those applicable to the search of a house, because an arrestee may be subjected to a full body search and the complete loss of liberty for up to forty-eight hours before seeing a judge—a far more disturbing experience than the search of a home. Yet in the case of arrests, the Court did not give priority to the warrant requirement. Instead, Justice Byron White, writing for the Court in *United States v. Watson*, assumed that the "ancient common-law rule" hinged entirely on the word "felony" and that it now permits a warrantless arrest in public places whenever the offense is given that classification.[8] This sort of "originalism," tied to a literal version of the original rule, not to its underlying principle, actually defeats rather than furthers the objectives that we know the Framers had in mind.

Another facet of the common law of arrest assumes great importance today—its limits on the use of force. The ancient rule barred the use of deadly force to capture a fleeing misdemeanor suspect but permitted deadly force to arrest a felon. Could federal agents therefore shoot to kill if Watson, the suspect in a credit card fraud, had spotted them and started to run? That hardly seems "reasonable" in today's world. But because the *Watson* decision accepted current offense labels as the basis for applying the eighteenth-century common-law rules, deadly force might be permissible even when a police officer pursues an ordinary shoplifting or purse-snatching suspect.

In a 1985 case, a fifteen-year-old Memphis teenager, Edward Garner, broke into a home late in the evening. When the police were called, he fled through the backyard. Just as he reached the fence, an officer commanded him to halt. Instead, Garner started to climb the fence. The officer, convinced that Garner was about to escape, opened fire. Garner suffered a bullet wound to the back of the head and died at the hospital later that night.

Garner's father sued the Memphis police for violating the Fourth Amendment. But because the boy's offense, a nighttime burglary, had always been classified as a felony, his claim seemed doomed; there was no doubt that in colonial times police were permitted to use deadly force to stop a fleeing burglary suspect. In this instance, however, the Court held the police action unconstitutional.

Justice White again wrote the opinion. But this time, after brief mention of the common-law rule, he concluded that reliance on this ancient but permissive standard "would be a mistaken literalism that ignores the purposes of a historical inquiry" and announced that "changes in the legal and technological context mean the rule is distorted almost beyond recognition when literally applied." The Court's majority therefore focused instead on practical considerations—the severity of the police action, the law enforcement goals that supposedly justified it, and the Court's own assessment of whether the use of deadly force was "a sufficiently productive means of accomplishing them." The Court concluded that it was "better" (the Court's word—an obvious value judgment) for some felony suspects to escape than for them to be killed, and that the use of deadly force to capture them is therefore "constitutionally unreasonable." The Court read the Fourth Amendment as permitting deadly force only when the fleeing felon threatens to inflict serious physical harm.[9]

Three dissenting justices would have allowed the use of deadly force in the *Garner* situation, but they, too, based their conclusion primarily on practical concerns. Like Justice White, they refused to be governed by the old common-law rule. Instead, they insisted that the "public interests justifying the conduct at issue here must be weighed against the individual interests implicated." They differed from the Court only in how they saw the "proper balancing of the interests."

Were all the justices wrong to set aside the specific rules and practices that the Framers considered "reasonable"? It is hard to see why "original intent" in this narrow sense should control in a world where its implications have changed so dramatically. Modern firearms are far more lethal, so officers who shoot are much more likely to kill. Yet the death penalty is much less acceptable than it was in 1792. In those days, all felonies were punishable by death, and long-term incarceration was not available as an alternative punishment because the prison as we know it had not yet been invented.* Today, in contrast, capital punishment is constitutionally forbidden for felonies that do not endanger life,[10] and even in murder cases, the death penalty can no longer be automatic.[11] To use deadly force to prevent a suspect's escape merely because there is probable cause to believe he committed a nonviolent felony now represents an utterly disproportionate response.

A Court that mechanically applied the eighteenth-century rule in these circumstances would therefore be *dis*honoring, not respecting, the Framers' values and intentions. So the justices were right in concluding (unanimously) that the case required them to *adapt* constitutional standards, in order to strike a balance that is reasonable under current conditions. No other approach would have kept faith with the Framers' commitment to imposing reasonable restraints on government power to intrude on the peace and security of the citizen.

Of course, that approach allows judges to interpret the Fourth Amendment in light of their personal sense of fairness (a favorite complaint of "originalists"). But a preference for judicial assessment over law enforcement discretion is a foundational principle of the Framers' own Fourth Amendment design. Trusting independent judges to make wise decisions was, they felt, far less dangerous than trusting officers to use their power wisely when deploying force without oversight. Nothing in modern circumstances gives us reason to question the wisdom of that judgment for our own times.

---

* Until the nineteenth century, jails in Britain and America served primarily as holding facilities for debtors and for inmates awaiting trial, corporal punishment, or execution. In 1790, Philadelphia Quakers began using a small local facility (the Walnut Street jail) for long confinement, but this remained a limited, experimental effort until Pennsylvania, still in the vanguard, opened a prison for extended incarceration of offenders (the Eastern State Penitentiary), the first of its kind, in 1829.

SEARCHING AND SEIZING PERSONAL EFFECTS

As we have seen, the warrant requirement is enforced very strictly for searches of the home but largely disregarded for felony arrests in public places. The amendment protects not only persons and houses but also papers and effects. What rule should govern the search of a traveler's suitcase? It can be a repository for private papers and possessions, but the need to shield it from intrusion certainly seems less acute than the need to protect the traveler's person, which can be seized and searched without a warrant whenever there is probable cause to believe him guilty of a felony.

After the *Watson* decision permitting warrantless felony arrests, the government argued that warrants should be required only for searches of the home, where privacy interests are at their peak, and that searches of luggage and other personal effects, like seizures of the person, should require only probable cause, not prior judicial approval. Yet in *United States v. Chadwick*, the Supreme Court, in an opinion by Chief Justice Warren Burger, rejected this suggestion.[12] Echoing William Pitt's defense of the humble tenement, the Court insisted that every container, however small or fragile, deserved the safeguard of judicial oversight. That conclusion makes sense because, as the Court emphasized, the warrant process plays an important role in preventing unjustified intrusions. But the upshot of *Chadwick* and *Watson* is paradoxical— the lowliest container, even a paper bag, is protected from interference by the requirement of prior judicial approval, but a person's body can be seized and jailed for up to forty-eight hours before a judge is required to review the issue of probable cause. Only the Court's wooden application of the common-law felony-arrest rule seems to account for this odd set of priorities.

And how, then, should the Fourth Amendment apply to cars suspected of transporting contraband? If police need a warrant to look inside a paper bag, surely the trunk of a car merits no less protection. Not so, said the Court. To search a *vehicle*, including its private repository areas, probable cause is sufficient; no warrant is required.[13] In explaining this result, the Court has emphasized that cars are mobile. But of course luggage is also mobile. For that matter, so is evidence hidden inside a house. In all these situations, police can freeze the scene until a warrant is obtained. Indeed, the home is the place where it is *hardest* to preserve the status quo, because occupants already inside must be evicted or kept under constant observation until the search warrant arrives. Most Fourth Amendment experts find it hard to reconcile the warrant requirement for homes, suitcases, and paper bags with the no-warrant rule for cars. The Court may be influenced by its perception of the practical challenges involved in immobilizing cars on the roadside while waiting for a search warrant. But if this explanation was ever plausible, it no longer makes much sense in light of the ability of today's police to obtain a "telephonic warrant," by calling an on-duty magistrate in roughly the same way that state and local police routinely call headquarters to verify license and registration.

And then there is the mobile home, a space that is far more private than a suitcase. Of course, a mobile home is, well, mobile. But even with its wheels, it is much easier to immobilize than the evidence in a large house. So what approach should the Fourth Amendment require? Is a mobile home more like a car or a house? To the surprise of many, the Court held that a mobile home will be treated like a car and that probable cause is therefore sufficient, without prior judicial approval.[14]

In decisions like these, the Court has shown little appreciation for the central place of the automobile in modern life. Americans spend far more time in their vehicles than our eighteenth-century ancestors could possibly have imagined. We routinely rely on the car's glove compartment, luggage areas, and other spaces for storage of our personal effects. While the Court has given no weight to this side of contemporary developments, it has uncritically assumed that evolving law enforcement needs render the warrant requirement impractical with respect to anything on wheels. The Court's willingness to adapt the Fourth Amendment to modern realities in this respect has been oddly one-sided.

SEARCHES INCIDENT TO ARREST

When an individual is arrested, the police routinely search his person and the area nearby, in order to disarm him and secure any evidence that he might destroy. This practice of "search incident to arrest" was apparently common in the eighteenth century and was permitted without a warrant, provided that the arrest itself was lawful. The upshot, however, is that police officers can sometimes conduct a fairly extensive search without prior judicial approval, either by arresting the suspect with an arrest warrant or by arresting the suspect in a public place with no warrant at all.

A 1969 case showed how easily the search-incident-to-arrest power can be abused. Officers went to the home of Ted Chimel to arrest him for the burglary of a coin shop. After taking him into custody near his front door, they searched the entire three-bedroom house, including its attic, garage, and workshop. In several rooms, the officers examined desk and bureau drawers and all their contents, looking for stolen coins. Without a search warrant, they conducted an intensive, top-to-bottom search that lasted almost an hour.

Although several prior decisions had permitted a search incident to arrest to extend to the "place" where the arrest was made, in *Chimel* the Court returned to first principles and imposed strict limits on the scope of searches incident to arrest. Reviewing the eighteenth-century history and the colonists' intense opposition to broad, general searches, the Court concluded that the requirement of a particularized warrant plays a "crucial part" in the scheme of the Fourth Amendment. Thus, in the absence of a warrant, searches of the home are "unlawful notwithstanding facts unquestionably showing probable cause," and exceptions from the warrant requirement are constitutionally permissible only when strictly necessary. In light of these principles, the Court held that a search incident to arrest must be confined to the immediate area that an arrestee can reach to grab a weapon or destructible evidence.[15]

The Court has continued to reaffirm this "grabbing area" limitation and has even tightened it to some extent. For many years, the Court gave the police great latitude after making an arrest on the highways. In *New York v. Belton* (1981), the Court held that after a suspect has been handcuffed and removed from his vehicle, the officer can continue to search the glove compartment and the entire passenger compartment, including the space under the car's back seat, even if there is no reason to believe there is any contraband or incriminating evidence to be found.[16] The *Belton* decision was sharply attacked for illogically placing law enforcement convenience over the motorist's privacy rights, and in 2009 the Court overruled it. In *Arizona v. Gant*, the Court held that once the driver and passengers are under the officer's control outside the car, a search of the vehicle over the objections of its owner requires reasonable grounds to believe that the car contains contraband or other evidence.[17]

SEARCHES WITH "CONSENT"

The Court's *Gant* decision, tightening the requirements for search incident to arrest, may have little practical effect, however, because the police can often accomplish the same result by invoking another useful law enforcement tool—the so-called consent search. After an officer makes a traffic stop, for example, it is not unusual for her to ask permission to check the trunk. Usually she will do so *before* making a formal arrest, so that the driver—still hoping to be let off with just a warning—will have every incentive to cooperate. The officer simply says something like "Mind if I have a look in the trunk?"

Most motorists acquiesce, but not necessarily because they are eager to give permission. More often they either fear the consequences if they object or believe that in any event they have no right to refuse. Indeed, in many cases the driver submits, knowing that when the officer opens the trunk, she will see a large bundle of drugs, packaged and stacked in plain view. In such circumstances, it is difficult to believe that the driver felt he had a meaningful choice.

Nonetheless, the Court has consistently held that mere acquiescence in these circumstances constitutes consent. Moreover, the officer is not even required to inform the citizen of his right to withhold permission.[18] The individual's consent is deemed valid as long as it is "voluntary," in the sense that it was not directly coerced. How "consent" can be considered voluntary when the citizen does not know he can withhold it is a mystery; the Court simply reasons that because society has an interest in conducting these searches, the officer should not have to give a warning that might encourage a citizen to object. The individual's constitutionally protected interest in the security of his papers and effects does not enter into the Court's equation.

EXCEPTIONS THAT SWALLOW THE RULE

Both of these exceptions to the warrant and probable cause requirements—the search incident to arrest and the consent search—have one important requirement: these tactics are legitimate only if the officer had legal authority to stop the individual in the first place. But in highway law enforcement situations, that prerequisite largely disappears because police can draw on a wide range of minor offenses to justify stopping and arresting almost any motorist. When a car's taillight is out, the driver can be arrested. When a car changes lanes without signaling, the driver can be arrested. When a car is clocked at a speed only one mile per hour over the limit, the driver can be arrested.

In situations like these, we ordinarily expect the officer simply to issue a traffic ticket (if she bothers to stop the car at all). But most states permit a full-custody arrest at the officer's discretion. And in *Whren v. United States* (1996), the Supreme Court held that such an arrest is permissible as long as the officer has probable cause to believe that an offense—any offense—was committed.[19] That arrest in turn carries with it the extensive "search incident to arrest" authority. The consequence is that even a minor traffic offense can result in a wide-ranging search of both the car and the driver, in the officer's unlimited discretion.

In the *Whren* case, plainclothes officers in an unmarked car followed the defendant because they had a hunch he might be selling drugs. But they had no probable cause to arrest him, and he did nothing suspicious while they tailed him. So in the end they pulled him over for making a turn without signaling. Once they arrested him for that offense, the search-incident-to-arrest authority allowed them to inspect the area within his reach, even though no evidence of the improper turn could possibly have been hidden in the car. When their inspection turned up two plastic bags of cocaine, Whren was arrested on drug charges. It made no difference that the traffic charge was an obvious pretext. As detectives on the *narcotics* squad, these officers had no interest in enforcing the motor vehicle laws; they had been assigned to drug-enforcement duties exclu-

MORE ESSENTIAL THAN EVER

sively. Nonetheless, Justice Antonin Scalia, writing for the Court, held that the sole test of Fourth Amendment "reasonableness" is whether there is probable cause to arrest for any offense whatever.

If a cocaine dealer like Whren does not elicit our sympathy, we must remember that for every instance involving a drug courier, there are countless police actions that never make the newspapers or the criminal court docket—instances in which law-abiding citizens guilty of nothing more than a traffic infraction are subjected to an intrusive but ultimately fruitless roadside search before they are permitted to continue on their way. Compounding the hassle and inconvenience, some motorists (minorities in particular) must endure these stops and searches repeatedly, with growing feelings of annoyance and humiliation. Yet, according to the Supreme Court, this tactic is perfectly legal.

Another case shows how far the Supreme Court is prepared to extend this sort of deference to law enforcement. In 2001, in *Atwater v. City of Lago Vista*, the Court held that a police officer did not violate the Fourth Amendment when he took a motorist into custody for failing to buckle her daughter's seat belt.[20] The officer had no suspicions of drug trafficking or other serious wrongdoing, and there was no incriminating evidence of any sort hidden in the car. Moreover, the seat-belt "crime" was punishable only by a fine, and the officer in this small town knew where to find the mother if she failed to pay. Yet the Court held that judges could not second-guess the police officer's decision to make a full-custody arrest, take the mother to jail and hold her there until she was able to post bond. Somewhat surprisingly, Justice David Souter, often a strong supporter of Fourth Amendment values, wrote the majority opinion, while Justice Sandra Day O'Connor spoke for the four dissenters.

Justice Souter's concern in *Atwater* was that allowing judges to reassess an officer's decision about when to make a custodial arrest would inevitably draw them into difficult and elusive questions of judgment. But as Justice O'Connor's dissent explained, the Fourth Amendment reasonableness inquiry need not be unmanageable. The reviewing court need only ask whether there was any legitimate justification for the officer's actions. In *Atwater*, the majority found no Fourth Amendment violation even though the officer offered no explanation at all.

More fundamentally, if the Court's bright-line rule ("probable cause is always enough") is designed to free the courts from difficult factual judgments, it stands our Fourth Amendment tradition on its head. As we saw in chapter 2, the central point of the amendment and the English law preceding it was to prevent arbitrary government action by ensuring that serious official intrusions do not escape judicial oversight. That framework was based on the express premise that decisions about searches and seizures should be made *by judges* whenever possible and *not* delegated to law enforcement officers. Our tradition has (until recently) been consistent and emphatic on this point.

The *Atwater* case is especially troubling not only because the Court upheld such an extreme assertion of law enforcement power, but also because the decision magnifies other search-and-seizure tools now in the police arsenal. In 1792, people spent relatively little time riding from place to place on horseback or in their wagons, and hardly any legal "rules of the road" governed them when they did so. A constable's authority to arrest on probable cause could rarely threaten the personal security they would expect as they went about their lawful daily activities.

Today, our lives are very different. Most of us are in our cars every day, often for hours at a time. And the motor vehicle code is so dense with requirements (many of them customarily honored in the breach) that it is scarcely possible to pass twenty-four hours without committing some sort of traffic infraction. In these circumstances, the power to effect a full-custody arrest merely on probable cause, regardless of how trivial the offense, allows officers to seize almost anyone they wish, with no meaningful judicial oversight. That power is daunting enough by itself, but it also carries additional authority for the arresting officers to search the individual's person and immediate surroundings at will. They also can "request" consent for an even broader search that most citizens assume they are obliged to allow. It is scarcely an exaggeration to say that, at least when we are driving, Fourth Amendment security exists largely at the discretion of the police.

There are many possibilities for abuse, but one that especially bears mention is racial profiling. Decisions like *Whren* and *Atwater* allow the police to stop and arrest any motorist, for any reason, provided a traffic violation has occurrred. They can selectively stop the drivers who are going fastest, those who seem drunk, or those who they think might be carrying drugs. They never need to explain the basis for their choices.

In theory, police officers cannot selectively stop a driver solely because he is black or Hispanic; that would violate the Fourteenth Amendment's equal protection clause. But as a practical matter, violations of equal protection are virtually impossible to establish in such circumstances. Part of the reason is that the Court's decisions do not categorically prohibit the police from taking race into account; officers can consider race when they have some *"nonracial reason"* for doing so. For example, the decisions permit police to consider race when it is part of the suspect's description provided by a victim; the decisions also permit them to consider race when they suspect that a particular offense (such as a killing that results from gang rivalry) was probably perpetrated by a person of a particular race.

The theory of these decisions is that the equal protection clause is violated only when state officials are motivated by racial animus and not when they are taking race into account for some other reason. In short, to establish an equal protection violation requires proof of discriminatory *purpose*, not just discriminatory *effect*. And this principle poses an almost insuperable obstacle to challenging racial profiling in law enforcement. An arrested motorist seeking to establish a denial of equal protection would have to produce evidence documenting the racial pattern of all other arrests the officer made, *as well as* the racial pattern in the arrests he *did not make*, because the motorist would have to prove that the officer had not arrested white drivers who were committing the same offense.

When the Supreme Court adopted its bright-line rule ("probable cause is always sufficient for arrest"), it responded to the concern about racial profiling with the assurance that any victim of that tactic would be entitled to bring an equal protection claim. But the reality is that unless an officer *admits* to making his arrests for racially discriminatory reasons, there is virtually no way to prove that highway stops are being made on that basis. The upshot is that whenever an officer has probable cause to arrest for a traffic infraction, no constitutional provision (as currently interpreted) prevents racial profiling.

That concern, if no other, provides a compelling reason to revisit the Court's overly simple assumption that probable cause is all the Fourth Amendment requires to justify an arrest. In the eighteenth century, the prerequisite of probable cause tightly restrained law enforcement discretion, but it imposes almost no limit on law enforcement discretion on streets and highways today. The Fourth Amendment requires *reasonable* police action and *meaningful* judicial oversight. Justice O'Connor's *Atwater* dissent pointed in exactly the right direction, a sensible and eminently simple solution: A traffic arrest should be held to meet constitutional standards only when there is some objective reason for taking the driver into custody.

THE EXCLUSIONARY RULE

A similar inversion of Fourth Amendment values—positing police trustworthiness and resisting judicial oversight—is reflected in the Court's recent attitude toward *remedies* for a Fourth Amendment violation. Early in the twentieth century, the Court adopted an "exclusionary rule," requiring federal courts to suppress evidence obtained in disregard of the Fourth Amendment.[21] Fifty years ago, in *Mapp v. Ohio*, the Court imposed the same requirement on the states.[22]

The exclusionary rule reflects two complementary concerns. One is deterrence—to compel respect for the Constitution by removing the incentive to disregard it. The other is what the Court in *Mapp* called "the imperative of judicial integrity." As Justice William Brennan later put it, suppression of tainted evidence "assur[es] the people...that the government would not profit from its lawless behavior, thus minimizing the risk of seriously undermining popular trust in government."[23] Justice Louis Brandeis stressed a similar necessity: "Our Government is the potent, the omnipresent teacher....If the Government becomes a lawbreaker, it breeds contempt for law;...it invites anarchy."[24]

In the 1970s, however, the Court began to deemphasize the judicial integrity rationale and announced that suppression was no longer an unqualified imperative. Instead, the exclusion of illegally seized evidence in any given case would be decided by "weighing the costs and benefits," with particular attention to the "substantial social costs" of suppressing reliable evidence that could help convict a guilty offender.[25] Initially, the cost-benefit calculus produced only a series of narrow exceptions to the exclusionary rule. But in the past five years, the Court has dramatically shifted its emphasis in conducting that analysis. The perceived costs of suppression have grown from "substantial" to "massive," and the Court now considers exclusion "our last resort, not our first impulse."[26] Taking that view one step further, the Court recently held that even police negligence in disregarding Fourth Amendment requirements will no longer require suppression in all cases; prosecutors are free to use illegally seized evidence unless the police misconduct is "sufficiently deliberate...and sufficiently culpable that [deterring it] is worth the price paid by the justice system."[27]

In explaining its reluctance to suppress the fruits of a Fourth Amendment violation, the Court claims that police officers generally can be trusted to obey the law. Casting the exclusionary rule and other tools of vigorous judicial oversight as the outgrowth of concerns unique to the 1960s, the Court portrays these doctrines as inauthentic, not legitimate reflections of the original Fourth Amendment tradition. Thus, the Court says, changes in urban politics, racial integration of police forces, and greater professionalism make obsolete many of the tools that the Warren and Burger Courts favored in response to police oppression of minorities. Now, the Court suggests, we can return to what it considers first principles.

On this subject as on so many others, the Court is once again turning our Fourth Amendment tradition and the commitments of the Framers inside out. The claim that law enforcement can be trusted to follow the law is of course politically appealing, and no doubt most police officers are persons of goodwill and decent intentions. Nonetheless, the premise that such probity will persist without independent checks, and that executive officers can be trusted to exercise search-and-seizure powers fairly, in the absence of judicial oversight, is precisely the assumption that the Fourth Amendment rejects.

To be sure, judicial oversight originally did not involve an exclusionary rule; the deterrent to an illegal search was the victim's ability to sue for damages. But by the early twentieth century, this remedy no longer had the bite that it did in the days of Otis, Entick, and

Wilkes. Police forces had grown enormously in size, influence and prestige; damage suits against them had become immeasurably more difficult. In practice, as Justice Frank Murphy wrote in 1949, "there is but one alternative to the rule of exclusion. That is no sanction at all."[28]

The Court's emphasis on racial progress is particularly odd and historically inapt. The Fourth Amendment at its inception had nothing at all to do with preventing racial oppression; the Framers, whatever their other virtues, were notoriously unconcerned with the problem of race. True, racial inequality in law enforcement began to claim greater attention in the 1960s—appropriately so. But the remedies the Court pursued—judicial oversight and constraints on discretion—were simply those that rule-of-law values and general Fourth Amendment principles required in any event, for all citizens. Nor is it plausible to suggest that racial inequities in law enforcement are now a thing of the past. There is no evidence to support (and much evidence to contradict) the Court's assumption that internal police discipline and civil damage liability provide all the incentives needed to ensure fair treatment.[29]

An even more revealing fallacy is the Court's view that suppression of illegally seized evidence inflicts "substantial" or "massive" costs. The Court spotlights the guilty offender who will (perhaps) escape conviction if illegally seized evidence cannot be used. Yet this cost—the cost to the prosecutor who cannot get access to incriminating evidence—is virtually inevitable in *any* system that produces compliance with the Fourth Amendment. The Court considers exclusion unnecessary because other remedies are supposedly sufficient to prevent violations. In fact, there is overwhelming evidence that other remedies are virtually toothless in the context of illegal searches and seizures. But if the Court's claim were true and other remedies were indeed sufficient to ensure compliance, the incriminating evidence in question would have been out of reach in any event, and precisely the same costs would be incurred. The costs the Court bemoans are simply the costs of adhering to Fourth Amendment requirements.

At bottom, the contemporary Court's hostility to the exclusionary rule cannot rest on discomfort with any particular remedy. It is a discomfort with the Fourth Amendment itself, and in particular with its regime of independent judicial control over law enforcement discretion.

That discomfort is doubly shortsighted, because—perhaps surprisingly—neither the exclusionary remedy nor even the substantive limits of the Fourth Amendment itself can fairly be seen as significant impediments to controlling crime. The original exclusionary rule rested on the Brandeis view that the *failure* to suppress breeds lawlessness. And criminal justice research provides compelling support for that insight; the evidence shows that official disregard for fair procedure weakens public willingness to respect legal requirements and cooperate with law enforcement efforts to apprehend offenders.[30]

As a consequence, relaxation of the exclusionary rule represents a direct assault on the capacity of our law enforcement system to maintain social order. At any given moment, a prosecutor's ability to use illegally seized evidence may help win a conviction—a tempting prospect for anyone whose overriding priority is to prevent crime. But focusing solely on that payoff in the case at hand is dangerously superficial. In the long run, the prosecutor's ability to use illegally seized evidence is likely to have exactly the opposite crime-control effect, because judicial tolerance for Fourth Amendment violations generates disrespect for authority, chills voluntary compliance, and discourages law-abiding citizens from offering the cooperation needed to catch and convict offenders in future cases.

In all these ways, the contemporary Court has allowed the Fourth Amendment to drift far from its traditional moorings. In most everyday law enforcement settings, its central principles of prior judicial approval and narrow constraints on official discretion no longer have much traction. Instead, government convenience and efficiency have become the controlling values, especially for searches and seizures outside the home. The right of the people to be secure in their persons and effects has a shape today that would be unrecognizable to the Framers.

...

CHAPTER FOUR

Policing Public Spaces

[S]trollers and wanderers may be going to or coming from a burglary.... The difficulty is that [strolling and wandering] are historically part of the amenities of life. [They have] encouraged lives of high spirits rather than hushed, suffocating silence. [Without] standards governing the exercise of...discretion...the poor and the unpopular [would be] permitted to "stand on a public sidewalk...only at the whim of any police officer." [T]he rule of law...evenly applied to minorities as well as majorities, to the poor as well as the rich, is the great mucilage that holds society together.

—JUSTICE WILLIAM O. DOUGLAS (1972)

...

IN THE EIGHTEENTH CENTURY, as we have seen, an arrest in a public place did not necessarily require a warrant. But a valid arrest always required probable cause to believe that the person to be seized had perpetrated a crime, and in the absence of an arrest, a valid search always required probable cause to believe it would yield contraband or the weapon used to commit an offense. Even as law enforcement evolved over succeeding generations, these rules continued to define the limits of permissible interference with personal liberty and privacy.

Over time, however, the reality on the ground changed dramatically. As American cities and towns grew in size, density, anonymity, and turmoil, a part-time constabulary of amateurs no longer sufficed. Full-time police officers, with expanding responsibilities, became essential instruments of local government. They disciplined unruly youth, kept order on the streets, and dealt with abusive drunks. Acting on behalf of local ward leaders, they distributed public benefits, ran soup kitchens, steered homeless immigrants to shelters, and doled out patronage. Through the nineteenth and early twentieth centuries, the pursuit and apprehension of criminals—the task for which search-and-arrest rules had been conceived—held a small place in the job description of the typical police officer. The police had become, in the words of one observer, "street corner politicians." And as this term implies, their positions often involved little objectivity, professionalism, or even job security. In the great tradition of the American spoils system, when a mayor or ward leader lost his position, the police officers he had hired were turned out as well.

Major waves of reform have transformed this regime, of course. The police have become professionalized, with a military style of leadership, specialized training, and guarantees of independence from city politics. But in one crucial respect, continuity outweighs change. Now, as in the past, apprehending criminals is a small part of police work. The job continues to center on maintaining order and delivering social services.

The police officer's carefully cultivated image as a "crime fighter," reinforced by television cop shows, has long obscured this point. But the fact remains that the average police officer, whether walking a beat or patrolling by car, spends most of his time on other problems—preventing congestion and disruptive behavior, controlling crowds, and helping citizens in need of assistance. Roughly two-thirds of all 911 calls involve requests for service or routine peacekeeping rather than crime prevention or detective work.

This orientation does not in itself pose Fourth Amendment difficulties. But the police are usually called on to render a particular kind of service. Although they deal with a broad array of social problems, the defining feature of their mission is the ability to address those problems by deploying nonnegotiable force. Whether an officer is asked to calm a boisterous drunk, break up a noisy late-night party, or help get a mentally disturbed person to the hospital, people "call the cops" when they need someone who can override disagreements quickly and impose a solution on the spot.

A social agency with this power is indispensable. But its existence clashes with important constitutional values. Our Fourth Amendment tradition sees unconstrained police discretion as a threat to liberty, and it therefore restricts the use of force absent probable cause to believe a crime has been committed. The problem, then, is to determine what limits should apply when police seek to maintain order by deploying physical force against citizens who have not committed any crime.

CONSTRAINING POLICE DISCRETION IN PUBLIC SPACES

Can an officer order an unruly teenager to leave a playground? (And who decides what behavior is "unruly"?) When a scruffy young man with baggy pants "lurks" in front of a jewelry store, can the officer require him to move away? If the man refuses (or leaves and comes back) can the officer arrest him for "loitering"? Can the officer search the man's pockets for a weapon, so that a possible robbery plan can be nipped in the bud?

Strict limits on these kinds of police activity could make it impossible to maintain order and forestall serious crime. Yet in the absence of limits, the police would be free to seize and search individuals whether or not there was any basis to suspect they had done anything unlawful. Well-dressed middle-class citizens might not be inconvenienced, but young people, the poor, those who dress in unconventional ways, and anyone who looks "out of place" in a neighborhood could be hassled by the cops. The "high spirits" Justice Douglas extolled, not to mention the essence of liberty as we understand it, would exist in public places only at the pleasure of the authorities. To keep faith with the Fourth Amendment's core commitments, we cannot leave government power of this sort unrestrained.

Yet, surprisingly, the Supreme Court's Fourth Amendment case law gave the police almost no guidance on these problems for more than a hundred years. Until 1868, the Fourth Amendment (along with the rest of the Bill of Rights) was applicable only to the federal government, not to the states and localities responsible for maintaining order on city streets. Most states had their own laws restricting searches and seizures, but these were seldom applied to routine peacekeeping functions. After adoption of the Fourteenth Amendment in 1868, the federal Constitution constrained local governments for the first time: it prohibited deprivation of liberty "without due process of law." But the Court did not immediately require states and localities to respect the specific requirements of the Fourth Amendment. It was not until 1961, when the Supreme Court first prohibited the use of illegally seized evidence in state criminal prosecutions, that local policing began to face Supreme Court scrutiny.[1]

The flashpoint was the order-maintenance tactic known as the "stop and frisk." When officers on patrol decided that someone should be checked out, they would push him against a wall and conduct an extensive pat down. If they discovered weapons or contraband, they would then have probable cause to arrest. But does the Fourth Amendment permit their initial actions, which were taken *without* probable cause? Police departments insisted that briefly grabbing someone by the shoulders and patting down his outer clothing was neither a "seizure" nor a "search" within the meaning of the Fourth Amendment.

A case from Ohio presented the issue to the Supreme Court. A Cleveland police officer, on afternoon patrol in the downtown shopping area, noticed a man walking back and forth in front of a store. Suspecting that the man might be "casing a stick-up," the officer confronted him, asked his name, and then quickly spun him around, patted his pockets, and recovered a pistol. At that point the man was arrested for possessing a concealed weapon. Although the officer did not have probable cause for the initial intrusion, the Ohio courts held that his pat down had not violated the Fourth Amendment.

The Supreme Court now confronted a dilemma. If the stop was a "seizure" or if the pat down was a "search," these police actions would require probable cause—a threshold that few order-maintenance practices could meet. But if the stop was not a "seizure" and if the pat-down was not a "search," then the prohibition of "unreasonable searches and seizures" would not apply at all, and these police actions would be constitutionally permissible, no matter how "unreasonable" they might be.

In *Terry v. Ohio*, one of its most important Fourth Amendment decisions, the Court found a way out of this predicament.[2] Because the officer's initial confrontation restrained the suspect's freedom of movement, Chief Justice Earl Warren, writing the Court's opinion, concluded that it had to be considered a "seizure" within the meaning of the Fourth Amendment. Nonetheless, because it was only a brief detention on the street, not a full-blown arrest involving a trip to the station house, it did not require probable cause, but only "founded suspicion"—an objective basis for believing that criminal activity requiring further investigation might be afoot. After that brief intrusion, however, any further restriction of the individual's freedom would be treated as an arrest and would be prohibited in the absence of probable cause.

The Court assessed the so-called frisk in a similar way. After describing standard procedures for a pat down ("The officer must feel with sensitive fingers every portion of the prisoner's body:... arms and armpits, waistline and back, the groin and area around the testicles, and the entire surface of the legs down to the feet"), Chief Justice Warren insisted that it was "sheer torture of the English language" to consider this intrusion as anything other than a "search."[3] Nonetheless, Warren observed, the outer pat down was less intrusive than a *complete* search, and it therefore could be justified by something less than full-blown probable cause. A limited frisk, he concluded, would be permissible when objective facts reasonably suggest that the suspect is armed and dangerous. This "frisk," however, is restricted to a pat down for weapons; any further exploration of the suspect or his possessions for drugs or other evidence of crime is prohibited in the absence of probable cause.

In a nutshell, the Court's key finding was that "the police are in need of an escalating set of flexible responses, graduated in relation to the amount of information they possess." The Court thus upheld the Cleveland police officer's actions. The objective circumstances—a suspect pacing back and forth in front of a store, repeatedly peering in the window, and then pacing back and forth again—created a reasonable suspicion that criminal activity might be afoot. And since a daylight robbery would require a weapon, the same circumstances supported a reasonable concern that the suspect might be armed and dangerous. The officer's response, in turn, was carefully tailored to the circumstances—a very short detention, with a limited outer pat down for weapons.

On its face, the *Terry* decision seemed to impose tight limits on the police officer's discretion. "The scheme of the Fourth Amendment," the chief justice declared, "becomes meaningful only when it is assured that... the conduct of those charged with enforcing the laws can be subjected to the more detached, neutral scrutiny of a judge who must evaluate the reasonableness of a particular search or seizure in light of the particular circumstances." This insistence on scrutiny of objective circumstances by a neutral judge echoes almost perfectly the traditional concern about discretion that the leading magistrates in England and influential voices like James Otis in the colonies emphasized in the eighteenth century (chapter 2).

Whether the *Terry* requirements constrain the officer as much in practice as they do in theory is a different matter. Judicial oversight of fast-breaking police actions on the street is far more difficult than scrutiny of warrant applications or other police measures planned in advance. And the standard that the police officer has to meet, "founded suspicion," is rather thin. Nonetheless, it is hard to imagine how the Court could have done better. As Chief Justice Warren said in *Terry*, "the wholesale harassment... of which minority groups, particularly [blacks], frequently complain, will not be stopped by the exclusion of any evidence from any criminal trial."[4] Despite the common misperception that its decisions had "handcuffed the police," the real Warren Court of 1968 was well aware of public safety needs and judicial limitations. It established a pragmatic framework of relatively flexible powers in order to preserve police capacity to maintain order in public spaces.

VAGRANTS AND MISFITS

The stop and frisk is only one of several devices police officers use to maintain order. Even more powerful are laws against "vagrancy" and "loitering." Regulations of this sort proliferated in sixteenth-century England and became widespread in common-law jurisdictions worldwide. In the original meaning, a vagrant was an able-bodied person who wandered from town to town without accepting employment. But over time, laws against vagrancy and loitering were extended to include all the unemployed, the homeless, and other "undesirables" who were present in public places.

After the Civil War, laws like these were widely used in the South to arrest newly freed blacks, who were then convicted of vagrancy or loitering and consigned to forced labor to pay off their fines. Even after the worst abuses of this system waned, vagrancy and loitering laws remained on the books throughout the United States, and they were often used to keep poor people, blacks, civil rights protesters, and others out of neighborhoods where they were unwanted in the eyes of the authorities.

Given the broad sweep of these laws, they afforded police officers a ready means for establishing not only "founded suspicion" but even the probable cause required to make a full arrest. A Florida ordinance, typical of the genre, provided for punishment of "rogues and vagabonds,...persons...strolling around...without any lawful purpose or object, habitual loafers, [and] persons neglecting all lawful business and habitually [frequenting] places where alcoholic beverages are sold." An Ohio law made it illegal to engage in conduct "annoying" to others. An Alabama ordinance made it "unlawful for any person to stand or loiter upon any street or sidewalk...after having been requested by any police officer to move on." Laws like these gave officers broad discretion to control the streets and arrest almost anyone who drew their disfavor. Fourth Amendment requirements were *technically* met, because officers could readily demonstrate probable cause to believe that a person on the street had committed these crimes: For example, the officer could simply testify that he himself had seen the person engage in "annoying" conduct, or had ordered the person to move on and had personally observed the person's refusal to do so. But the Fourth Amendment's underlying purpose—to impose objective limits on law enforcement—was thoroughly defeated. The problem was simple: the Fourth Amendment by itself imposes no constraint on *what* can constitute a crime.

To fill this gap, the Court turned to the Fourteenth Amendment's requirement that "no State shall...deprive any person of...liberty...without due process of law." The Court had long held that this principle renders any law "void for vagueness" if it leaves the average citizen unable to know what it prohibits or if it authorizes arbitrary law enforcement. In *Papachristou v. City of Jacksonville*, the Court concluded that the Florida vagrancy ordinance failed this test and was therefore unconstitutional.[5] The Ohio law was not ambiguous in the same way, because the word "annoying" has a well-understood meaning. But the Court nonetheless held it void for vagueness, because this meaning depends on the subjective reactions of the police and other observers rather than on any objective behavior.[6] The Alabama antiloitering law posed a different problem. Because it permitted arrest only after an officer had asked an individual to move on, it gave the citizen unambiguous notice of what the authorities expected. But the Court nonetheless held the law unconstitutionally vague because it gave no guidance *to the police.*[7] The Court reasoned that an officer cannot constitutionally be granted discretion to tell citizens what to do, on pain of arrest for noncompliance with his orders. In these decisions, the Court preserved the core Fourth Amendment value of personal security by permitting official interference with liberty only when police have reasonable grounds to believe an individual is violating an objectively clear law.

This clarity requirement will seldom impede truly legitimate law enforcement, but it does come under attack from time to time. In the 1980s and 1990s, concern about urban unrest and decay surged in response to the crack epidemic, the growth of inner-city gangs, and a sharp escalation in youth violence. New police-management theories suggested a link between minor disorder ("broken windows") and the incidence of serious offenses. Many academics, local politicians, and residents of blighted neighborhoods claimed that the police needed more flexibility when seeking to maintain order in public spaces. Many also saw the *Terry-Papach-ristou* restrictions on police discretion exclusively through the lens of American race relations and the civil rights movement of the 1960s. Forgetting that comparable limits on law enforcement had been a constant of English law for centuries, they argued that black voting power in the cities and the racial integration of urban police forces rendered these Warren Court decisions outdated.

As support for more assertive policing grew, many localities enacted or more actively enforced low-level public-order offenses (e.g., jaywalking, littering), youth curfews, antiloitering laws, and the like. A 1992 Chicago ordinance declared it unlawful for two or more people to remain at street corners, parks, and other public places with "no apparent purpose," if a police officer suspected any of them to be a "gang member" and told them to disperse. The law—aimed at gangs that congregated on sidewalks to deal drugs and control their "turf"—was aggressively implemented. Over a three-year period police ordered over eighty-nine thousand individuals to disperse and arrested over forty-two thousand people on charges of "gang loitering" when they failed to move away quickly enough. Many middle-class citizens saw initiatives like this as a good way to "take back the streets." Yet an accumulating body of research demonstrated that such tactics were not reducing crime and, to the contrary, were triggering resentment and mistrust of law enforcement among at-risk youth, who most needed to be steered in positive directions.

City officials were slow to react to these social science findings, but in the meantime, legal challenges to the ordinances proliferated. Some of the new public-order laws seemed to permit just the kind of loose police discretion that Warren-era precedents had condemned. Supporters of the laws acknowledged that problem but felt the time had come to declare that tight limits on police discretion to maintain order in public spaces were no longer a constitutional imperative.

The Supreme Court, however, held in *City of Chicago v. Morales* that the gang-loitering ordinance was void for vagueness.[8] Justice Clarence Thomas, in a forceful dissent, argued that "to perform their peace-keeping responsibilities satisfactorily, the police inevitably must exercise discretion."[9] But six justices found the Chicago effort unacceptable because it gave officers unlimited discretion to determine what activities constituted "loitering." The Court reaffirmed the principle that statutes must provide clear standards to govern police authority to stop, search, and arrest.

To many, this is illogical because the police in any event exercise enormous discretion in deciding whether to arrest people who jaywalk, litter, or drive just over the speed limit. But the crucial point is that citizens in those situations always have a safe harbor— they can preserve their freedom of movement simply by not littering, not speeding, and not violating other widely disobeyed but clear laws. If instead the police could decide where the line of permissible conduct falls, personal security from government interference would quickly evaporate.

The irony is that such broad law enforcement powers, though superficially attractive for the police, do not ultimately help control crime. Over the past two decades, research has established that any short-term deterrence benefit gained by fear of police sanctions is offset when heavy-handed tactics alienate the members of targeted communities, chilling their respect for authority and their willingness to help apprehend suspected offenders in their neighborhoods.[10] Justice Douglas, quoted at the outset of this chapter, could not have been aware of these social science findings, but they powerfully vindicate his insight that the rule of law is "the great mucilage" holding together the diverse and potentially antagonistic elements of our society.

EXCHANGING PLEASANTRIES AND INVITING
(OR COMPELLING) COOPERATION

Whether helping a person in distress, maintaining order in a crowded park, or keeping a lookout for serious crime, the cop on the beat does not always need to exert force. Officers often chat informally with possible witnesses. When they approach a potential suspect, their most effective tactic may simply be to ask low-key, nonconfrontational questions rather than to immediately initiate an aggressive frisk.

The *Terry* decision acknowledged that encounters between police and private citizens are sometimes little more than what the Court called "friendly exchanges of pleasantries."[11] Truly voluntary interactions obviously should not be restricted by the Constitution. Only when police assert their authority over an individual does the Fourth Amendment, with its requirement of "founded suspicion," come into play. But how do we know whether any particular encounter is merely an "exchange of pleasantries" or is instead an exercise of an officer's authority, backed by a threat of force?

The Warren Court insisted that there is a "stop" (which requires founded suspicion) "whenever a police officer accosts an individual and restrains his freedom to walk away."[12] If the officer orders a person to halt and grabs him by the collar, a forcible stop obviously has occurred. But what if the officer merely *asks* a person to stop? ("May I speak with you a minute?") Should the legal result turn on whether the officer intends to prevent the person from walking away or on whether the person *thinks* he is free to walk away?

Terry did not resolve this question. It does not seem reasonable to hold the police responsible every time an unusually sensitive citizen feels intimidated. The problem is quite different, however, if the officer's behavior would lead *an ordinary person* to assume he is being ordered to submit. Officers can fairly be expected to know how ordinary people will interpret their actions and to adjust their conduct accordingly—specifically, to back off and leave the individual at peace unless they have an objective reason to suspect wrongdoing.

For a few years after the *Terry* decision, the Court followed this approach, requiring police officers to demonstrate grounds for suspicion in situations where "a reasonable person would have believed that he was not free to leave."[13] Subsequent rulings, however, have greatly diluted this prerequisite.

A 1984 case involved federal raids conducted in hopes of catching undocumented immigrants. In each instance, some agents had guarded the exits of a factory, while others (a force of fifteen to twenty-five altogether) moved systematically through the shop floor, showing their badges and questioning employees to determine their immigration status. The agents had no objective grounds to suspect anyone of violating the law—indeed, most employees were U.S. citizens of Hispanic descent or immigrants working lawfully on proper visas. If the agents had constrained their "freedom to walk away," their Fourth Amendment rights were clearly violated. But in *INS v. Delgado*, the Court held that the agents' tactics were permissible. Justice William Rehnquist, writing for the Court, insisted that despite the manner in which the team of agents had occupied the factory, workers being challenged as potential "illegals" had "no reason to believe that they would be detained... if they simply refused to answer."[14]

Justice Rehnquist's opinion illustrates an approach the Court has used with increasing frequency—setting a theoretically appropriate standard but directing the lower courts to apply it in a way that bears little relationship to social or psychological reality. In *Delgado*, federal agents were watching the exits, and the officers inside were not exchanging casual pleasantries. They projected authority, deliberately so, and did nothing to indicate that the workers could decline to cooperate. As Justice William Brennan noted in dissent, the record established "a frightening picture of people subjected to wholesale interrogation under conditions designed not to respect personal security and privacy, but rather to elicit prompt answers from completely intimidated workers."[15] Whatever a legal expert might have understood about her rights in these circumstances, ordinary citizens (not to mention recent immigrants with limited knowledge of our language) would certainly feel constrained to remain in place and respond to questions. Brennan was by no means unfair when he observed that the Court had assessed the facts with a "studied air of unreality" in order to reach a conclusion "rooted more in fantasy than in the record of this case."[16] By severing the notion of a forcible seizure from the everyday reactions of ordinary people, and by ignoring the impact of tactics deliberately crafted to create an impression of authority and constraint, the Court gave officials broad power to intrude on the average person's sense of freedom in public places, without any need for justification or judicial oversight.

In recent decisions, the Court has deployed this approach to afford ever greater leeway to law enforcement. Regardless of circumstances, citizens approached and questioned by a police officer on the street are supposed to know that they can ignore the officer, turn their backs, and walk away. If they do not do so, the Court assumes that they are cooperating of their own free will.

A striking example is the Court's treatment of police efforts to obtain a person's "consent" for a search that the law does not permit an officer to conduct without the person's permission. Agents might consider an individual suspicious and want to search on the basis of unacceptable considerations like his race. Or they may simply want to search everyone in sight, in hopes of finding someone in possession of contraband. Either way, they have no right to compel cooperation; they must have *voluntary* consent.

One police tactic for obtaining consent has been developed especially for use in the "war on drugs." Narcotics officers board an interstate bus at a scheduled stop. Having no reason to suspect any passenger, they walk down the aisle, asking each passenger to consent to a search of her luggage. Usually no one refuses. These travelers supposedly "consent" to a police search of private belongings that people usually prefer to shield from strangers, and—most surprisingly—they even "consent" when there are large quantities of drugs to be found.

Of course, the passenger's decision to acquiesce in this kind of search is not really mysterious. She is trapped in a confined space with an armed officer hovering over her. It is almost impossible for her to leave the bus, and if she could do so, she would be left stranded at a remote highway rest area when the bus leaves. Although the officers "ask" to search, they do not tell the passenger she can refuse, and their actions clearly signal that with or without cooperation, they intend to inspect every piece of baggage on the bus.

In theory, a refusal to consent should not by itself provide grounds for a search. But how many passengers know this? In any case, the common-sense assumption (that the passenger has little choice in the matter) is largely accurate. A traveler's refusal to consent will inevitably make the officer more suspicious and increase his determination to question her. The ordinary passenger, even a relatively sophisticated one, will reasonably assume that refusal to cooperate will land her in trouble. Of course, the officers hope that everyone will submit peaceably, but passengers usually have little doubt that the officers intend to search everyone's luggage, by force if necessary.

Is a search permissible if a passenger gives "consent" in these circumstances? One reasonable answer would be that most travelers believe they have no right to obstruct the officers and therefore that their acquiescence is merely a submission to authority, not a truly voluntary choice. But this is not the answer the Supreme Court has given. Instead, in majority opinions by Justices Anthony Kennedy and Sandra Day O'Connor, the Court has held that a bus passenger's consent is valid in these situations.[17] Drawing on the *Delgado* case, the Court simply posited that the "reasonable person" knows he can disregard the police "request." Therefore, in the absence of aggravating circumstances (such as an officer pointing his service revolver), the failure to object renders the search voluntary. Because the Court assumes that the police have done nothing to constrain the passenger's freedom of choice, the searches are permissible without any objective suspicion of criminality and without any notice to the passenger that she is entitled to refuse consent.

OBJECTING CITIZENS LOSE TOO

Over the past two decades, the Court has reduced judicial oversight of police actions even when officers demand submission explicitly.

In *Hodari*, a 1991 case, police officers grew suspicious of a group of black teenagers clustered around a parked car. When the officers approached, the youths scattered. In no uncertain terms, the officers ordered them to halt, but the teens kept running. Just before a pursuing officer reached him, one of the boys tossed away a small rock of crack cocaine. The officer apprehended him and arrested him on drug charges.

This encounter was certainly no "friendly exchange of pleasantries." In addition, unlike the interstate bus searches, the officers in this instance *demanded* obedience, and the drugs were discovered as a direct result. But the Court nonetheless held that the order to halt did not count as an intrusion on Fourth Amendment rights.[18] Because the Fourth Amendment is addressed to "seizures," the Court said, it does not necessarily restrict a mere *attempt* to seize.

In parsing the constitutional language, Justice Antonin Scalia's opinion for the Court conceded that the word "seizure" includes unsuccessful attempts to seize an individual by *physical* means, like grabbing a suspect who breaks away. But he insisted that the word's ordinary meaning cannot extend to unsuccessful *verbal* attempts: "a policeman yelling 'Stop in the name of the law!' at a fleeing form that continues to flee is no seizure." Therefore, Justice Scalia reasoned, when verbal commands are resisted, they fall outside the Fourth Amendment, and the police are not required to show any basis for issuing them. As a result, the crack obtained by ordering the youth to halt was admissible, even though the officer had no legitimate justification for making that demand.

The Court's distinctions—between attempted seizures that succeed or fail and between those that are physical or verbal— reflect an exceptionally literal method of constitutional interpretation. Is this approach nonetheless acceptable (perhaps even admirable) as a demonstration of rigorous thinking and good lawyerly analysis? A Court consistently committed to close parsing of constitutional text would of course consider not just the word "seizure" but *all* the words of the Fourth Amendment, which begin by guaranteeing "the right of the people to be secure in their persons." The proper textual question, therefore, is whether a citizen justifiably feels that officials are intruding on his personal "right...to be secure" when an armed police officer orders him to halt.

The Court did not consider that question, but there can hardly be any doubt that the officer disturbed the teenager's tranquility and freedom of movement. The infringement is obvious when an individual submits to the order. One might argue that the citizen who walks away has not lost his liberty—he is still moving. But the Fourth Amendment does not protect only the physical capacity to move; it protects—literally—the "right to be secure." And an order to halt deeply disrupts a person's sense of security, even when he tries to disregard it.

The Court did not deny this. Rather, instead of considering psychological realities, it focused on the association of the word "seizure" in English usage with "a laying on of hands or application of physical force to restrain movement." Under that definition, there is no "seizure," and thus no need for justification, even when an officer says "Stop or I'll shoot!" The *Hodari* decision instructs us that no Fourth Amendment interest is affected—that the "right to be secure" is not impaired—even when an officer threatens to kill an individual who is merely exercising his constitutional right to walk away. There is not even a Fourth Amendment intrusion when the officer starts shooting, unless the bullets hit their target, for only then is there the equivalent of a physical "laying on of hands." Yet those absurd conclusions follow directly from *Hodari*'s holding that Fourth Amendment protection is limited to seizures involving either submission to authority or physical restraint.

Fidelity to constitutional text sometimes requires courts to reach odd results, but this is not one of those occasions. The same insistence that the Fourth Amendment protects only against *physical* intrusions once led the Court to hold that wiretapping was not a "search" and that conversations, unlike tangible effects, could not be "seized." The Court abandoned those formalistic interpretations forty years ago[19] and has never looked back; it recognizes that electronic surveillance can be a search without any physical intrusion (chapter 6). Justice Scalia himself has authored two leading decisions that reaffirm this point.[20] The *Hodari* rule thus does not reflect a genuine commitment to strict textual interpretation but only an arbitrary, unexplained set of distinctions: *searches* do not require a physical intrusion, but some seizures do; seizures of *personal effects* do not require physical means, but seizures of *the person* do.*

Logic-chopping decisions like *Hodari* unfortunately have become commonplace. One last example will underscore how far the Court has gone in relaxing oversight of police interference with liberty on the streets.

Unless officers demand compliance, their interactions with citizens are normally treated as "exchanges of pleasantries" because the Court assumes that people will terminate unwanted encounters; we supposedly know we have a right to continue on our way unless the police have an objective reason to intrude. But in 2000, the Court held that citizens *do not* have an unqualified right to avoid encounters with the police, even when the officers have no basis for

---

* In a footnote in *Hodari*, Justice Scalia acknowledged that the Fourth Amendment governs attempts to seize *effects*, even when no physical means are used. He offered no reason to treat persons differently from their effects, and of course this distinction is just as artificial as the distinction between successful and unsuccessful attempts to detain or between physical and verbal attempts.

ordering cooperation. Chicago police officers had converged on a corner where drug dealers sometimes hung out, and several men ran off. The officers gave chase and tackled them. When the officers initially approached, they had no grounds to suspect the men of misconduct and therefore no justification for chasing and seizing them. But Chief Justice Rehnquist, writing for the Court, said the very fact that the men tried to leave gave the officers "founded suspicion" sufficient to authorize the forcible stop.[21]

The decision rested once again on finespun logic that in practice negates the Fourth Amendment right to freedom of movement. In theory, individuals have an absolute privilege to walk away from police who do not have an objective basis for detaining them. This privilege is the essence of liberty. Indeed, the Supreme Court itself relies on this privilege—and assumes that all individuals are aware of it—when it concludes that those who do not walk away must have *chosen* to remain.

To avoid this inconvenient point, the Court insisted that "unprovoked flight is not a mere refusal to cooperate" and that flight is especially suspicious in a "high-crime area." The upshot is that when police who lack objective suspicion approach a person and ask for information, the person need not cooperate, but he cannot make his unwillingness too emphatic. *Leaving* is permissible; *fleeing* is not.

Again, a wholly artificial distinction cuts away an essential pillar of Fourth Amendment freedom. To be sure, some young men may run from an approaching squad car to avoid being caught with drugs or weapons. But they may also run when they have nothing to hide, simply because they do not want to be hassled. And being in a "high-crime area" hardly changes the equation. That qualification may simply provide a means to ensure that constitutional protection for personal security on the street remains intact in middle-class urban and suburban communities. In any case, whatever the Court may have meant by a "high-crime area," minority men in such neighborhoods are *especially* likely to fear contact with the police, even when they have done nothing illegal. Of course, an individual on the street in a high-crime area may be committing some offense. But if the Fourth Amendment means anything, a person's age, his race, and the place where he lives cannot make him fair game for suspicionless police searches and seizures. Whatever an area's crime rate, the great majority of its inhabitants are not criminals.

Unfortunately, the public often applauds decisions that reject Fourth Amendment claims in these circumstances, even when the Court's reasoning is preposterous. After all, the defendant is almost always a "bad guy" caught red-handed with drugs or a concealed weapon. But when police who have no reason for suspicion board a bus and search every passenger, twenty or thirty innocent travelers are inconvenienced, and the privacy of their luggage and personal effects evaporates. When agents occupy the shop floor of a factory, block the exits, and question all the workers, dozens who are innocent of any wrongdoing are subjected to anxiety and stress. Every time police chase down and tackle a group of teenagers hanging out on a street corner, the officers alienate, frighten, and physically overpower six or eight blameless kids along with the offender they occasionally catch. Analysis of street stops in New York City has shown that African Americans are six times more likely to be stopped than whites and that less than 11 percent of all stops yield any incriminating evidence. In other words, roughly 90 percent of those stopped and frisked are innocent citizens needlessly subjected to distress and humiliation.[22]

This collateral damage is seldom visible when Fourth Amendment challenges come before the courts, because the only individual likely to raise a constitutional claim is the one facing prosecution. But where methods like these are part of the law enforcement arsenal, law-abiding citizens must live with virtually unrestricted police discretion to intimidate and harass innocent people in public places. To describe such an environment as a "police state" will seem an exaggeration to those who do not encounter such tactics on a regular basis. But these methods, now endorsed by the Supreme Court, affect thousands of citizens every year, undermining their security, their respect for authority, their sense of acceptance in the wider community, and even their willingness to assist law enforcement efforts to control crime.

No doubt such police conduct would be perceived differently by most Americans if it touched their own lives. In practice it rarely does, because tactics like these are almost always focused on low-income neighborhoods and places where minorities and the poor typically congregate. As a result, for many of our law-abiding but politically powerless fellow citizens, the peace of mind, freedom of movement, and protection from government intrusion that the Fourth Amendment was designed to guarantee have been deeply eroded. Ironically, the Court's recent decisions do not even serve their ostensible crime-control purpose. Far from making it easier to preserve order, they usually have the opposite effect, because they do so much to weaken the mutual trust that sustains the stability of a law-abiding society.

CHAPTER FIVE

The Administrative State

Experience should teach us to be most on our guard to protect
liberty when the Government's purposes are beneficent.... The
greatest dangers to liberty lurk in insidious encroachment by men
of zeal, well-meaning but without understanding.

—JUSTICE LOUIS BRANDEIS (1928)

. . .

IN THE ROW HOUSES and apartment towers of urban American, fire
marshals and building inspectors often seek to search entire groups
of homes on a routine basis, in order to check the safety of their
electrical wiring and other systems. And city officials have long
believed that a requirement of probable cause to suspect dangerous
conditions in a particular home would make the building code virtually unenforceable. Responding to that view, the Supreme Court has
held that health and safety inspectors can enter homes and apartments without permission, by using an "area warrant" issued for an

entire neighborhood on the basis of some neutral enforcement principle.[1]

As we have seen, however, the Fourth Amendment provides that "no warrants shall issue, but upon probable cause," and probable cause has always meant objectively grounded suspicions of criminality focused on a particular person or place. The area warrant is nothing more than a modern name for the dreaded general warrant that the Fourth Amendment was meant to forbid. Was the Court therefore wrong to permit area inspections by fire marshals?

A committed believer in enforcing the "original intent" of the Framers presumably would have to take that view. But the contemporary area warrant addresses problems the Framers could not have imagined—urbanization, population density, and essential but potentially dangerous modern amenities like electricity and indoor plumbing. Some adaptation of strict eighteenth-century rules, therefore, cannot be precluded out of hand.

Many people believe that the idea of a "living constitution" only *expands* individual rights and causes democratic government to lose flexibility. But as the issue of fire safety inspections reveals, the dynamic character of our Constitution can also have the opposite effect—permitting government to exercise broader search-and-seizure powers than the Framers themselves accepted.

Respect for the Fourth Amendment in a changing society requires the Court to make allowance for problems that were unknown in the eighteenth century. But the Court must also adhere to the amendment's central commitments: sheltering private spaces from unjustified government intrusion, denying unbounded discretionary powers to the executive, and assuring judicial oversight. This is "originalism" tightly harnessed to the vision of the Framers but adapting the legal details in order to achieve their underlying goals effectively under new circumstances.

Within that framework, it is by no means easy to establish appropriate, logically consistent standards to govern searches that seem to differ in some way from conventional criminal investigations. The problem is not confined to fire safety inspections, because over the past half century, "administrative" scrutiny of homes, offices, personal effects, and even peoples' bodies has proliferated to the point where many Americans encounter these searches regularly at work, in schools, at the airport, on the highways, or in trains and buses. The once obscure administrative search doctrine now matters enormously in our daily lives. Yet the Supreme Court has never indicated precisely which features must be present in order for an "administrative" search to be constitutionally permissible.

In *Camara v. Municipal Court*, Justice White, writing for the Court, declared that area warrants to inspect for fire hazards were justified without any individual suspicion because "the public interest demands that all dangerous conditions be prevented or abated, yet it is doubtful that any other canvassing technique would achieve acceptable results."[2] This reasoning has intuitive appeal, but its limits are hard to discern.

Suppose that building inspectors want to visit homes in a low-income neighborhood to see whether any of them is being used as a "crack house." Suppose they want to check apartments in a public housing project to find out where firearms are being stashed. Should they be able to enter these residences merely on the authority of an "area warrant"—without any showing of probable cause that any particular apartment contains illegal drugs or weapons? What if a city wants to stop drivers on the highway and take samples of their blood and urine to determine whether any of them is using drugs or alcohol? Or suppose that police want to search all houses in a neighborhood in order to locate a fugitive suspected of murder. All these situations pose potential threats to community health or safety. And all of them can be said to meet the vague *Camara* criteria—that "the public interest demands" that a dangerous condition be prevented and that enforcement techniques requiring probable cause may not achieve "acceptable" results. A moment's reflection makes clear that traditional Fourth Amendment requirements could quickly become irrelevant if the government can escape them merely by claiming a plausible need for additional flexibility in order to achieve "acceptable" results.

The *Camara* Court also insisted that fire safety inspections, unlike conventional searches, involve a "relatively limited" invasion of privacy because they are "neither personal in nature nor aimed at the discovery of evidence of crime." Searches for drugs, firearms, or murder suspects obviously do not fit that description. But fire safety inspections do not fit that description very well either. A safety inspection of the home is inevitably intrusive. The inconvenience can become extensive if inspectors choose to examine conditions in rooms throughout the house. Violations discovered can trigger criminal charges, but even if criminal prosecution is ruled out, why should that fact give officials more leeway to disturb the occupant's privacy? Why should law-abiding citizens have less protection than suspected criminals? As an appellate court observed in a pre-*Camara* decision refusing to relax Fourth Amendment standards for these inspections, "to say that a man suspected of crime has a right to protection against search of his home without a warrant, but that a man not suspected of crime has no such protection, is a fantastic absurdity."[3]

Even so, most legal scholars share the intuition that fire safety inspections should not require probable cause. A closer look at the details of *Camara* helps explain why. Several circumstances (none decisive in itself) combine to justify some exception to traditional Fourth Amendment requirements. One is that the public safety concern (the risk of fire in an urban setting) is not only substantial but almost impossible to address in other ways; for practical purposes, there is *no less intrusive alternative.* Whether or not current efforts to combat murder and drugs produce "acceptable" results, *some* level of enforcement is feasible with ordinary methods of investigation, because criminal offenses usually leave some trail of observable facts. This is not the case with dangerous heating, plumbing, and wiring conditions; most housing code violations cannot be detected from outside, and often they are not apparent even to the residents themselves. If housing code inspections were to require probable cause, they might not be possible at all.

A second crucial factor is that homeowners targeted for fire safety inspections are selected under a systematic plan based on *neutral criteria*; they are not chosen because of suspicions directed against them personally. This fact does not lessen the intrusion on their privacy, but it reduces significantly the stigma and indignity that typically accompany searches based on individual suspicion. Neutral criteria also help prevent harassment of individuals and other abuses of discretion. And when all citizens face the same risk of being searched, the burden is widely shared, and there is a more effective political check on unreasonable, abusive, and unnecessary inspection regimes.

A third factor in the mix is the paradoxical point that the inspections do not seek evidence of crime. At first blush, this explanation for the result in *Camara* seems odd, because it implies that citizens not suspected of misconduct deserve fewer privacy safeguards than suspected criminals do. And in any case, fire safety standards and other administrative regulations are usually backed by criminal sanctions; mere regulation and criminal law enforcement seldom can be neatly disentangled. But the absence of a dominant *prosecutorial purpose* is relevant in much the same way that neutral criteria are. When law enforcement goals are uppermost, the pressures for official overreaching, the risks of abuse, and the need for an independent check are at their peak. And a search for evidence of a criminal offense typically involves a frightening confrontation between the citizen and armed, hostile officers. In contrast, if prosecutions are precluded (and to a lesser extent if prosecution is little more than a theoretical possibility), feelings of anxiety, resentment, and fear are much less likely, even if some intrusion on the homeowner's privacy inevitably remains.

In short, some relaxation of traditional Fourth Amendment restrictions is justifiable when there is a substantial concern for the public welfare, no less intrusive way to address it, a systematic inspection system based on neutral criteria, and the absence of a prosecutorial purpose. The especially strong safeguards that the Framers considered essential to prevent abusive law enforcement searches are much less necessary when all these prerequisites are met. In such cases, warrants based on probable cause need not be required.[4]

Even so, the need for some shield against an unduly intrusive government does not disappear. Searches and seizures must always be "reasonable," and citizens obviously should retain this safeguard even when they are not suspected of any criminal offense. The Fourth Amendment therefore requires careful judicial oversight even for regulatory inspection programs that meet the requirements for "administrative search" treatment. An independent judicial assessment, as the Framers contemplated, can ensure that regulatory inspections do not intrude on individual privacy in ways that are unnecessary or disproportionate to the social welfare problem being addressed.

The fire safety inspections at issue in *Camara* met these requirements, and the Court was therefore justified in upholding them. Yet in subsequent decisions, the Court has permitted administrative searches that are far less faithful to Fourth Amendment principles. The Court has upheld inspection programs where government needs are weak and a probable cause requirement is by no means unworkable. It has allowed some "administrative" searches that are conducted by police rather than civilian inspectors and some that are based on suspicion of individuals rather than neutral criteria. Ostensibly "regulatory" programs have sometimes passed muster even when their goals mix public safety concerns with substantial possibilities for criminal prosecution. Over time, the Court has gradually discarded most of the limits that justified flexibility for inspections like those in *Camara*.

In place of those limits, the Court has established only a loose framework for judicial oversight. The Court does insist that in order to escape the strict traditional regime of Fourth Amendment safeguards, an administrative search must serve "special governmental needs, beyond the normal need for law enforcement."[5] But the Court often permits conventional crime control functions to be repackaged as acceptable "special needs." Once a "special need" is shown, moreover, the Court usually gives extraordinary weight to ordinary administrative convenience when it rules on whether the inspection program strikes a "reasonable" balance between privacy concerns and government objectives.

To be sure, the Court has not given carte blanche to regulatory inspections; it occasionally rejects arguments for relaxed administrative search treatment, even in regimes where civilian inspectors have no discretionary powers. But, paradoxically, the Court has *upheld* "administrative" searches in which police officers exercise broad discretion and collect evidence for use in criminal prosecutions. In the absence of any limiting principle, administrative search decisions have been even more erratic than other Fourth Amendment rulings. But the general pattern of the past two decades has predominated in this area as well. The Court has repeatedly sacrificed protection from government intrusion to unconvincing claims for ease and efficiency.

FROM PUBLIC SAFETY TO ADMINISTRATIVE CONVENIENCE

Claims for flexible administrative search treatment are especially strong when public health or safety is put at risk by latent conditions that will remain undetected if authorities can inspect only with probable cause. *Camara* involved a problem of just this sort. Dangerous conditions in factories, mines, and stone quarries pose similar difficulties. And the federal regulatory regimes established in these settings carry the same kinds of safeguards as the fire safety program in *Camara*. They rely on routine inspections triggered by neutral criteria rather than individual suspicion, they are designed for prevention rather than criminal law enforcement, and they are structured to keep disruption and intrusion to a minimum. With those features in place, the Court has properly upheld them.[6]

In contrast, when the justification for an administrative search is slender and far removed from a specific health or safety concern, the Court should be willing to hold the inspections unconstitutional, even if they use routine procedures based on neutral criteria. In a few instances, the Court has done just that. A 1990 Georgia statute required all candidates for state office to provide certification that they had tested negative for illegal drugs. The state asserted that the prospect of a drug user running successfully for office would "undermin[e] public confidence and trust in elected officials." In *Chandler v. Miller* (1997), the Court rejected this argument, holding that "where... public safety is not genuinely in jeopardy, the Fourth Amendment precludes the suspicionless search, no matter how conveniently arranged."[7] Of course, valid administrative searches are not limited only to those in the "public safety" category. The Court's essential point was simply that Georgia's objectives lacked the concreteness and weight of a direct threat to community health or safety; the state's goals were, the Court said, merely "symbolic" and not "*important enough* to override the individual's acknowledged privacy interests."[8] The Court assessed the *significance* of an alleged regulatory concern and properly demanded that it be substantial in relation to the privacy interests that the inspections would infringe. Unfortunately, decisions like *Chandler* are rare. Insistence on a substantial need to protect public safety has more often given way to acceptance of government objectives remote from any concrete safety concern and barely distinguishable from conventional law enforcement.

In *New York v. Burger* (1987), the Court upheld a statute that authorized unannounced, warrantless searches of the business premises and office records of automobile scrap companies, in order to discourage auto theft and enable authorities to trace stolen vehicle parts.[9] The inspections were carried out solely by police officers; there was no claim that conventional methods of investigation were infeasible and no claim that the stolen auto parts posed any threat to public health or safety. The principal objective was simply to catch (and prosecute) those implicated in receiving stolen goods; indeed, the police officers involved in the case conceded that their sole purpose was to gather evidence of a crime. Nonetheless, Justice Harry Blackmun, writing for a five-to-four majority, upheld the regime as "properly administrative," dismissing the concerns about police involvement on the ground that auto theft was "a serious social problem" and that penal and regulatory objectives often coexist in comprehensive state solutions.[10]

The *Burger* decision, with its expansive conception of the administrative search category, was strongly influenced by the fact that the target of the inspections was a regulated business, not a residence. But just a week later, in another five-to-four decision, the Court extended the same permissive approach to the search of a private home.

Joseph Griffin was on probation after conviction for disorderly conduct. A probation officer thought "there...might be guns in

Griffin's apartment." Possession of a gun would, if confirmed, violate Griffin's probation; it would also, because of his prior record, constitute a serious crime. The officer, relying on a state regulation permitting warrantless inspection of probationers' homes, searched the apartment without any objective basis for his suspicions, and a handgun he found was used to convict Griffin of a weapons-possession felony. This was no routine inspection according to neutral criteria and, unlike the inspections in *Burger*, it did not affect only business premises. It was a search for evidence of a crime, in a residential context where ordinary methods of investigation can be—and often are—used to develop probable cause. Indeed, the case involved *none* of the circumstances that had previously served to justify relaxed Fourth Amendment requirements. Nevertheless, in *Griffin v. Wisconsin* (1987), the Supreme Court upheld the intrusion as a valid "administrative" search.[11]

In an opinion by Justice Antonin Scalia, the Court's majority concluded that the probation system "presents 'special needs' beyond normal law enforcement" because effective supervision of probationers helps assure their rehabilitation.[12] And the Court found the usual search-and-seizure rules "impracticable"[13] because the warrant process could cause delay, the probable cause standard would heighten the evidentiary burden, and these requirements in turn could reduce a misbehaving probationer's fear of being caught—all consequences inherent in the Fourth Amendment's traditional system of safeguards. The Court did not simply treat the sacrifice of Griffin's privacy as part of the punishment for his earlier offense but instead permitted the goal of more effective surveillance to qualify as a "special need" and found the traditional process for establishing probable cause "impracticable" as applied to ordinary criminal conduct. With the prerequisites for an "administrative" search diluted to this extent, slender justifications can support inspections affecting the general public as well. A wide range of checkpoints, drug testing programs, and other inspection regimes have won approval as a result.

TRAVEL CHECKPOINTS

Stops and searches at fixed checkpoints were becoming common in American life long before 9/11, and for many years the Court has given police great latitude in deciding when and how to operate them. Occasional instances of judicial disapproval are the exceptions in a sea of rulings that accept everyday expediency as sufficient justification.

Because roadblocks and metal detectors at airports subject everyone passing the checkpoint to roughly the same inconvenience, the possibilities for racial profiling and similar abuses are greatly reduced. But they are by no means eliminated, because police retain considerable discretion in deciding where such checkpoints are needed. All agree that metal detectors are appropriate at airports. But where should a roadblock be placed to catch drunk drivers or drug couriers? The possibilities are wide open, and low-income, politically powerless neighborhoods are especially likely to be chosen.

In any case, as with Georgia's drug tests for political candidates, equal treatment alone does not satisfy Fourth Amendment concerns. Government intrusion on security and privacy undermines freedom and requires justification, even when a large class of citizens bears the burden equally. As Justice Sandra Day O'Connor concluded after exploring the colonial history on this point, "protection of privacy, not evenhandedness, was then and is now the touchstone of the Fourth Amendment."[14]

The Court rightly acknowledges this principle and has condemned some checkpoint stops and searches even when all travelers face the same intrusion. Indianapolis police instituted a program of roadblocks to intercept drug couriers. Drivers were detained for no more than five minutes and were not searched but subjected only to a "sniff" of their vehicles by a dog trained to detect narcotics. Yet because the city's objective was drug interdiction, a conventional law enforcement purpose, the roadblock's justification was one that traditional Fourth Amendment requirements have always taken into account. And the law enforcement purpose created distinctive dangers of overreaching, with a distinctive potential for arousing anxiety and fear. Travelers should not suffer this restriction on their freedom of movement in the absence of objective grounds to suspect wrongdoing. For those reasons, the Court, in an opinion by Justice O'Connor, properly held the Indianapolis checkpoint program unconstitutional.[15]

In contrast, airport metal detectors focus on prevention rather than prosecution. Rather than attempting to trap criminal offenders unawares, they aim only to stop travelers from taking dangerous items on board, and passengers have ample opportunity to discard unacceptable material before approaching the screening point. Because such programs do not seek evidence for criminal prosecution and address a substantial safety concern that cannot be met through searches on probable cause, they are properly assessed under administrative search standards. Even so, an airport screening program that permitted unguided discretion in selecting individuals for scrutiny or used needlessly invasive inspection techniques would be unreasonable and therefore unconstitutional. The airport screening systems that most citizens now take for granted have been upheld only because they screen everyone routinely on the basis of neutral criteria and (at least in theory) intrude on privacy no more than necessary.

Unfortunately, the Court has accepted checkpoint programs that fall far short of satisfying these standards. Immigration enforcement is one example. In the attempt to stop the entry of undocumented immigrants, federal agents operate checkpoints not only at the border but also on nearby roads that bring immigrant workers to the cities. In theory, all travelers passing through the checkpoint should face the same initial treatment—an agent is supposed to stop them for one or two minutes and perhaps ask them a few brief questions. Only those travelers who arouse suspicion are to be detained longer and subjected to a more intensive interview. Even so, the obligations imposed on all travelers—to stop and undergo the initial law enforcement interrogation—are intrusive in themselves. A major problem, moreover, is that the individuals who get even greater scrutiny because they arouse suspicion (perhaps because of their apparent ethnicity) will usually be citizens who have committed no crimes. Detaining and interrogating them at greater length exposes lawful residents to inconvenience and indignity, perhaps on a daily basis. In addition, unlike fire safety inspectors and airport security personnel, border patrol agents typically want to *prosecute* many of those they catch. But the Court held that because the "primary" goal is to deport rather than prosecute the illegal immigrants, immigration checkpoints serve a "special need," and the stops therefore qualify as permissible "administrative" seizures.[16]

"Sobriety checkpoints" pose a similar problem. Michigan police established highway roadblocks to stop and question motorists in order to spot signs of drunk driving. Like weapons that a passenger might take onto an airplane, drunk driving can pose a life-threatening danger. But an impaired motorist often can be identified by observation (something that is difficult or impossible in the case of a potential hijacker), so conventional law enforcement methods have considerable value, and there is no imperative need to stop and inconvenience every driver on the road. Moreover, the Michigan roadblock, like the immigration checkpoints, sought to detect wrongdoing (a purpose that makes the stops inherently more disturbing), and when drunk drivers were discovered, they were charged accordingly. Nonetheless, in 1990 the Supreme Court, in a six-to-three decision, accepted this tactic as a valid "special needs" program. Chief Justice William Rehnquist, writing for the Court, concluded that the law enforcement objectives were secondary and that the program's "primary" goal was to get drunk drivers off the road.[17]

This approach makes Fourth Amendment safeguards turn on an elusive, largely theoretical distinction between "primary" and "secondary" purposes. The sobriety and immigration checkpoints affected drivers in exactly the same way as the Indianapolis's narcotics checkpoint. But the first two were permissible because criminal prosecution was considered a subsidiary aim of the law enforcement officers in charge. It takes little imagination for authorities to design a roadblock that can pass muster under that standard, whatever their real motivation.

To serve as a faithful guardian of our Fourth Amendment tradition, the Court must exercise much closer oversight of government efforts to inspect persons and property at roadblocks and other travel checkpoints. Absent an extraordinary, life-threatening emergency (a report of a terrorist truck bomb about to detonate, for example), the core values of the Fourth Amendment require objective, individualized justification when law enforcement officers conduct stops and searches that carry a significant prospect of criminal prosecution. Justice Clarence Thomas, the Court's most insistent "originalist," has recognized this point clearly. "I rather doubt," he has said, "that the Framers of the Fourth Amendment would have considered 'reasonable' a program of indiscriminate stops of individuals not suspected of wrongdoing."[18] The Court's more permissive approach allows police far more leeway than necessary and takes from the traveling public an important part of our traditional "right...to be secure" from government intrusion.

DRUG TESTING

Laboratory analysis of urine samples is familiar to most adults who see a doctor, but privacy implications change dramatically when government authorities use such tests for their own purposes. Testing of the sample can reveal the use of medications associated with innocent but highly personal conditions—physical, mental, and emotional. Requiring someone to disclose the contents of his body to the government is at least as intrusive as requiring him to disclose the contents of his luggage. Analysis of a compelled urine specimen therefore involves an obvious Fourth Amendment "search." And the individual's privacy is affected even before that stage, because the authorities and the person to be tested (unlike a doctor and her patient) are in an adversarial relationship. In order to prevent cheating when the fluid sample is given, the authorities often insist on close personal observation—another "search."

The best way to guarantee the integrity of a urine sample is direct frontal observation when the person tested provides it. The procedure for obtaining the fluid specimen can be made less intrusive—for example, by indirect observation or better yet (for the person tested) by allowing her to give the sample in a closed bathroom stall. But every step that makes collection of the sample less invasive also makes the test more vulnerable to manipulation. Drug users can obtain "pure" samples (widely available on line), and they can acquire devices that bring substitute samples up to body temperature and mimic the sounds of normal urination. Unless the process for collecting the sample is highly intrusive, drug users usually can find ways to circumvent it. So why bother subjecting nonusers to the loss of privacy inherent in the laboratory analysis and the inevitably disturbing specimen-collection procedures?

Occasionally, the Court has appreciated these problems and refused to approve regimes for mandatory drug testing. In South

Carolina, for example, medical personnel took blood and urine from all pregnant women who sought treatment at a city hospital, and a lab then tested the samples for drug use. The program had a significant public health rationale (early treatment for the babies of drug-addicted mothers), and the invasion of privacy was no worse than in drug testing programs the Court had approved, for example for railroad employees involved in fatal train accidents.[19] But in the South Carolina regime, law enforcement played a prominent role. Although police were not involved in taking or analyzing the fluid samples, prosecutors had helped design the test protocols, with an eye to prosecuting expectant mothers for endangering their fetuses or "delivering" cocaine to them. Because the primary purpose of the program was to facilitate law enforcement, the Court rightly held in *Ferguson v. City of Charleston* (2001) that the tests were unconstitutional in the absence of a warrant and probable cause.[20]

In one instance, the Court invalidated a drug testing regime even without prosecutorial involvement or the targeting of low-income minorities. In *Chandler*, the Georgia election law case mentioned earlier, candidates for public office who tested positive had the option to withdraw from the race, and test results were not available to prosecutors. In addition, the individuals subjected to testing were well placed to exert political influence, and democratic processes therefore could be expected to work reasonably well in assessing the costs and benefits of the program. But because the testing requirement infringed the privacy of the unwilling minority and did not address a truly significant problem, the Court properly held the regime impermissible.[21]

Cases like *Chandler* and *Ferguson* are exceptions, however. The Court has usually upheld drug testing regimes even when "special needs" and program benefits were slender. The Court's approach to drug testing programs in public high schools has been especially permissive.

IN LOCO PARENTIS?

Broadly speaking, minors enjoy constitutional rights very similar to those of adults. They are guaranteed freedom of speech and religion, due process of law, and protection from unreasonable government searches and seizures. Police who search teenagers on streets or in parks violate the Fourth Amendment if they cannot show probable cause (chapter 4).

What, though, of searches of minors conducted when they are in school? We have long since rejected the old idea that public school officials automatically stand "in loco parentis," with all the authority that parents can exercise over their children at home. After all, children are required to attend school, and while there, they are subject to rules that their parents may find abhorrent. Harsh punishments, disrespect for privacy or personal dignity, and other mistreatment by public officials are no more acceptable in school than elsewhere. Indeed, these abuses are especially troublesome in school, because they bear down on a captive audience. If a teacher's behavior warps the child's sense of justice or respect for authority, those consequences can shape attitudes toward the police and the law itself throughout adult life. The Fourth Amendment thus plays a vital social role when it restrains the power that officials exercise over minors at school.

Even so, the constitutional rights of children in public schools, like the rights of adults in other government settings (for example, in courthouses or in the military and other public employment), are not identical to constitutional rights elsewhere. Officials can restrict student speech that seriously disrupts the educational process, even though the First Amendment would fully protect equivalent statements made on a street, in a park, or on a home computer. Likewise, school authorities can justifiably restrict students' Fourth Amendment rights to some extent, if necessary to preserve an orderly educational environment. Teachers and administrators need some leeway, but judges have an important oversight function, and the Court will therefore condemn searches of schoolchildren that are "excessively intrusive in light of the age and sex of the student and the nature of the infraction."[22] Absent extraordinary circumstances, for example, a "strip search" is unconstitutional, "even with the high degree of deference that courts must pay to the educator's professional judgment."[23]

A carefully conceived drug testing regime can properly pass muster under this approach, but the Court has also approved extremely broad, needlessly intrusive programs. In *Veronia*, for example, the Court held in 1995 that a public school could require student athletes to undergo urinalysis tests as a condition of participating in any high school sport.[24] Justice Scalia, writing for the Court, emphasized that athletes volunteer to take part in the activity and know that privacy in the locker room is inevitably scant. But those facts do little to temper the intrusiveness of having a school official supervise the student when he provides a urine specimen, and they do nothing at all to mitigate the privacy concern arising from laboratory analysis of the sample. It could hardly be said that adults who shower in the locker room of their sports club have waived their Fourth Amendment protection from government-mandated urinalysis tests.

Justice Scalia also mentioned the potential safety problem posed when drug use causes playing-field injuries to drug-impaired athletes or their competitors. But this worry, however valid for football or wrestling, has little application to sports like tennis or golf. Even with respect to football, testing of all participating students is normally unproductive and unnecessary; direct observation of a student's performance is a less intrusive and far more effective way to detect signs of drug impairment.

That said, schools have a responsibility to verify the fitness of students who risk serious injury in contact sports, and officials seeking to meet that obligation deserve some leeway. The Court must grant them a degree of deference while still exercising an effective oversight role. Thus, a program for searching athletes' lockers for drugs would be too poorly targeted to warrant judicial deference; such searches simultaneously expose too much (all of the students' personal effects) and too little (drugs that students keep and use outside school). In contrast, urinalysis testing restricted to athletes participating in contact sports—with protocols to limit the dissemination and use of test results—would be narrowly focused and could properly be upheld as "reasonable," even if the justices themselves might consider such a program unnecessary.

But just as a regime for random inspection of the backpacks of football players could not be deemed reasonable, a narrower type of search, limited to urinalysis, cannot be considered reasonable when extended to students who want to compete on the golf team. For purposes of preventing sports-related injury, the *Veronia* testing policy was preposterously overbroad. As Justice O'Connor noted in dissent, "the [school district's] suspicionless policy of testing all student athletes sweeps too broadly, and too imprecisely, to be reasonable under the Fourth Amendment."[25]

In the end, Justice Scalia acknowledged that the school district's program had a more wide-ranging motivation. Because the school district believed that athletes were leaders in the student body's drug culture and set an influential example, it targeted them for testing in part in order to make drug use less attractive for *all* students. Its concern was not just to protect athletes from injury but also to discourage unhealthy behavior among students generally. Yet if this goal justifies invasive searches of student athletes without individual suspicion, mandatory urinalysis testing presumably could be extended to all public school students.

Subsequent Supreme Court decisions move even closer to giving school officials a sweeping power of that sort. The community of Tecumseh, Oklahoma, required drug tests for middle school and high school students who wished to participate in *any* extracurricular activity. The policy was challenged by Lindsay Earls, a member of the choir, the marching band, and the National Honor Society. Rejecting her claim in *Board of Education v. Earls* (2002), the Court's opinion, by Justice Clarence Thomas, maintained that students choosing these and other activities had to accept a loss of privacy because the activities are "competitive" and because "some of these clubs and activities require occasional off-campus travel and communal undress."[26] Although drug use in *Earls* did not pose a risk of playing-field injury, as it did for some of the sports in *Veronia*, the Court equated the two programs, claiming that "the health and safety risks identified in *Veronia* apply with equal force to Tecumseh's children" because "the nationwide drug epidemic makes the war against drugs a pressing concern in every school."[27]

Despite that point of similarity, however, the justification for the testing regime in *Earls* was far more tenuous. The choice to take part in competitive sports, which triggered the testing obligation in *Veronia*, can reasonably be considered voluntary, but as Justice Ruth Bader Ginsburg noted in her dissent in *Earls*, participation in *some* extracurricular activity is "a key component of school life, essential in reality for students applying to college, and…a significant contributor to the breadth and quality of the educational experience."[28] Moreover, the *Veronia* Court had attributed great significance to the loss of privacy that inevitably attends participation in high school sports. As we have seen, the *Veronia* decision gave this facet of the testing program far more weight than it deserved, but in *Earls*, the Court strained credulity in equating the athletic locker room to the setting in which other extracurricular activities occur. Whatever the relevance of communal shower facilities to the privacy issues at the heart of urinalysis drug tests, there is no remotely comparable loss of privacy in activities like choir and band.

Beyond these contrasts, health and safety concerns are properly paramount, and in that regard the two situations have virtually nothing in common. As Justice Ginsburg noted, "competitive school sports [unlike choir and band]...expose students to physical risks that schools have a duty to mitigate." Supporters of the Tecumseh policy tried valiantly to identify a potential for harm in other activities, citing "the risk of injury to a student...handling a 1500-pound steer (as [Future Farmers of America] members do) or working with cutlery or other sharp instruments (as [Future Homemakers of America] members do)."[29] Justice Ginsburg was properly dismissive of this far-fetched argument: "Notwithstanding nightmarish images of out-of-control flatware, livestock run amok, and colliding tubas,"[30] the great majority of students subject to the testing policy were not engaged in any safety-sensitive activities whatsoever.

Ironically, students who take part in extracurricular activities are less likely to develop substance abuse problems than their less engaged peers. So the Tecumseh policy was doubly wrongheaded. It invaded the privacy of students who pose the fewest problems and deterred the most at-risk students from participating in wholesome activities that might alleviate their attraction to drugs. That the Court, in the guise of maintaining a "balance between the schoolchild's legitimate expectations of privacy and the school's equally legitimate need to maintain [the learning] environment,"[31] was willing to uphold such an ill-advised program does not bode well for the future of the Fourth Amendment.

Administrative searches with flexible prerequisites are sometimes necessary and legitimate. But government officials have relentlessly sought new authority for checkpoint and inspection regimes that needlessly sacrifice the privacy of citizens not suspected of any wrongdoing. The Court's tendency to accept such programs, often for the sake of nothing more than ease and efficiency, leaves Fourth Amendment safeguards in a precarious state for a broad range of ordinary activities in our daily lives.

. . .

CHAPTER SIX

Wiretapping, Eavesdropping, and the Information Age

The progress of science in furnishing the Government with means of espionage is not likely to stop with wire-tapping. Ways may some day be developed by which the Government, without removing papers from secret drawers, can reproduce them in court, and by which it will be enabled to expose to a jury the most intimate occurrences of the home.... Can it be that the Constitution affords no protection against such invasions of individual security?

—JUSTICE LOUIS D. BRANDEIS (1928)

. . .

ACROSS A WIDE RANGE of government activity—searches, arrests, policing the streets, protecting public health and safety—the Supreme Court has failed to understand the Fourth Amendment's central goals or has failed to take them seriously. Often the Court has insisted on retaining eighteenth-century rules under radically different modern circumstances or has crafted new rules driven by law enforcement need, with little attention to the risks of abuse and the need for oversight. In the late 1960s, the Warren Court and the early Burger Court encountered modern technology in cases that drew the justices out of this sorry pattern. But that hopeful moment proved to be short-lived.

EAVESDROPPING

When the Fourth Amendment was written, the invention of the telephone lay almost a century in the future, but eavesdropping was not unknown. (In colonial times, the snoop would listen by hanging beneath the eaves.) The amendment's Framers, though familiar with that practice, chose language that grants protection only to "persons, houses, papers, and effects" and requires search warrants to specify "the things to be seized." As a result, when investigators in the early twentieth century turned to wiretapping as a law enforcement tool, constitutional protection for private conversation was uncertain.

Prohibition brought the issue to a head. Roy Olmstead headed a syndicate that was importing illegal liquor into the United States. Without getting a warrant or showing any basis for their suspicions, federal agents tapped the phone lines to his house and listened to his telephone conversations with associates. But the Supreme Court held that Olmstead could not object to this tactic, because there had been no "search" and no "seizure." Chief Justice William Howard Taft acknowledged that the agents would have needed a warrant to open and read letters that the conspirators had sent through the mails. But tapping their phone conversations was different, he said, because the constitutional text protected only "material things." A letter "is plainly within the words of the amendment.... The letter is paper." In contrast, he said, when the agents tapped Olmstead's phone, "evidence was secured by the use of the sense of hearing and that only. There was no entry."[1] And as a result, no Fourth Amendment safeguards were available at all.

The question presented in *Olmstead* thus had significance far beyond that of any issue we have previously encountered. In the preceding pages, we have seen countless difficulties and disagreements concerning the proper reach of Fourth Amendment protection: When are probable cause or objective grounds for suspicion necessary? When must officers get judicial approval in advance? What police tactics are "unreasonable" under all the circumstances? But the upshot of *Olmstead* was that wiretapping was not subject to *any* Fourth Amendment limits. When the Court concludes that government actions involve no "search" and no "seizure," there is no judicial oversight before *or after* the fact, and police tactics cannot be found to violate the amendment, *no matter how unreasonable* they may be. The concern throughout this chapter, exemplified by *Olmstead*, is therefore the most basic of all—to determine when any form of Fourth Amendment protection can come into play.

Responding to Chief Justice Taft's conclusion in *Olmstead*, Justice Brandeis, speaking for four justices, wrote what was to become his most famous dissent. He conceded that when the Fourth Amendment was adopted, "force and violence were then the only means known to man by which a Government could directly [violate privacy]." But, he continued,

> time works changes....Subtler and more far-reaching means of invading privacy have become available....Writs of assistance and general warrants are but puny instruments of tyranny and oppression when compared with wire-tapping.... The makers of our Constitution...knew that only a part of the pain, pleasure and satisfactions of life are to be found in material things. They sought to protect Americans in their beliefs, their thoughts, their emotions and their sensations. They conferred, as against the Government, the right to be let alone....To protect that right, every unjustifiable intrusion by the Government upon the privacy

of the individual, whatever the means employed, must be deemed a violation of the Fourth Amendment.[2]

Even in 1928, Taft's formalistic reading of the Fourth Amendment was scarcely tenable. Two centuries earlier, English judges had understood that the value of a person's documents lies not in the physical paper but in the information they contain. "Papers," the court said in *Entick v. Carrington* (1765), "are often the dearest property a man can have. [They] will hardly bear an inspection; and...where private papers are removed and carried away, the secret nature of those goods will be an aggravation of the trespass."[3]

Unconvincing from the start, the Court's conclusion in *Olmstead*—that a search requires a physical intrusion and that a seizure occurs only when agents take "material things"—became increasingly fragile. In one case, federal agents entered an area next to an office and placed a microphone against the wall (a "slap mike") so that it amplified sound from the adjoining room. The Court held that this was not a search because there had been no physical entry into a protected space.[4] But when agents used a "spike mike" that penetrated the wall, the Court held that there *was* a search.[5] That result left Fourth Amendment law in shambles, because the privacy of the home is disturbed to the same extent, regardless of which kind of microphone the government uses. As Justice William O. Douglas noted in a concurring opinion, "The depth of the penetration...is not the measure of the injury."[6]

The holding in *Olmstead* had become—literally—paper thin, and in *Katz* (1967) the Warren Court overruled it. "The Fourth Amendment," Justice Potter Stewart said for the Court, "protects people, not places."[7]

Charles Katz had placed a call from a public phone booth, and agents had monitored his end of the conversation by placing a slap mike against the outside of the cabin. The surveillance did not affect Katz's home or personal papers, and it involved no physical penetration of any private space. Even so, the Court stressed that a person who uses a public telephone "is surely entitled to assume that the words he utters into the mouthpiece will not be broadcast to the world. To read the Constitution more narrowly is to ignore the vital role that the public telephone has come to play in private communication."[8]

PROTECTING PEOPLE, NOT PLACES

The *Katz* decision was a big leap forward, and not just because it extended constitutional safeguards to wiretapping and the spoken word. More important, *Katz* put to rest the formulaic brand of originalism that prior Courts had invoked to stifle Fourth Amendment safeguards. The *Katz* Court held that the amendment must be applied in light of its underlying purpose; courts must interpret it to serve that purpose effectively in changing conditions.

And the Court did not focus solely on *technological* change. Only a mindless originalism would insist that because airplanes were unknown in the eighteenth century, Congress's power to regulate interstate commerce cannot extend to them. It is therefore not a large step to afford Fourth Amendment protection against electronic devices that enable police to "enter" a home without physically penetrating its walls. But in order to reach the surveillance used against Katz, the Court needed a different sort of flexibility, because the eavesdropping occurred in a public place, where eighteenth-century citizens did not expect protection from prying eyes and ears.

The decisive developments in *Katz* were social as much as scientific. What made the surveillance troubling was not just the new technology but changes in everyday life, specifically "the vital role that the public telephone has come to play in private communication."

The *Katz* decision was a watershed because the Court recognized that people were living differently and that the privacy the Framers cherished was taking different forms. The Court saw that Fourth Amendment values can be at risk regardless of the place where surveillance occurs and regardless of the means used: "What a person knowingly exposes to the public, even in his own home or office, is not a subject of Fourth Amendment protection.... But what he seeks to preserve as private, even in an area accessible to the public, may be constitutionally protected." In the shorthand formula now widely accepted, constitutional safeguards are mandated whenever the government intrudes on a "reasonable expectation of privacy."[9]

This Fourth Amendment concern can arise without a physical trespass and even without reliance on sophisticated technology. A police officer obviously violates reasonable expectations if he climbs into a crawl space over a public toilet and uses that vantage point to observe people using the bathroom stall. All of us have a "reasonable expectation" that we will not be spied on in this way.

To be sure, the "reasonable expectation" test cannot give mathematically precise answers. In that respect, it reflects the words of the Fourth Amendment itself. The right "to be secure" and the prohibition against "unreasonable" searches express values that a democratic society and its courts must protect under constantly evolving circumstances. That much should not be controversial. But how, in practice, can courts determine what "reasonable expectations of privacy" actually are?

Judges and academics often find it natural to answer that question by looking to the actual expectations of reasonable people in contemporary American society. But this point of reference cannot be decisive. An amendment intended to protect dissidents and social outcasts must not be read to permit whatever intrusions are acceptable to those in the conventional mainstream. And even mainstream expectations can fall short of what the amendment must cover. Suppose the government announced that from now on it was going to collect, store, and analyze all email sent from any computer in the United States. Once such a practice was publicized, we could no longer expect these messages to remain private. But the police can hardly be allowed to obliterate the Fourth Amendment so easily. Existing expectations are shaped by the police practices that the law allows. If we decide what the law allows by looking to existing expectations, we end up chasing ourselves in a circle. Inescapably, decisions interpreting the Fourth Amendment determine what kind of privacy we are *entitled* to expect.

If the Court is to make that judgment conscientiously, it cannot draw answers exclusively from old common-law rules, read with wooden literalism. Yet as we shall see, the Court's decisions applying *Katz* have continued to do just that, with results that too often defeat the very goal the Framers themselves intended to realize—a vibrant democracy that leaves room for individuals to enjoy personal and political independence. "Modernization" cannot be a one-way street where the government benefits from new technologies while citizens are left with no protective buffers other than those that sufficed in 1791—the roofs, walls, and sealed envelopes that afforded complete privacy in the eighteenth century.

Although the justices cannot legitimately apply old rules while ignoring their contemporary effects, it is equally illegitimate for them to render constitutional judgments not tied to our Fourth Amendment tradition at all. They cannot simply grant whatever surveillance powers (or impose whatever safeguards) they themselves consider desirable. They cannot give the police freedom from oversight just because they think that oversight is not worth its costs. Their decisions must remain anchored in the constitutional text and in the values it was meant to preserve. We know that the Fourth Amendment aims to guarantee every citizen the opportunity to claim areas of life that can be insulated from unrestricted government spying. We know that the Framers saw such spying as a potentially fatal threat to individual autonomy and political freedom. The justices remain faithful to their responsibilities only when they seek to identify safeguards that, in modern conditions, permit each citizen to shield intimate matters from official eyes and ears.

KEEPING PACE WITH TECHNOLOGY

In the years since the *Katz* decision, the Supreme Court has never questioned its holding that electronic eavesdropping of a public phone booth is prohibited in the absence of a warrant. Indeed, the Court could hardly abandon this conclusion without disregarding conceptions of constitutionally protected liberty that are now universally shared, thanks to the understanding of modern privacy that the Warren Court articulated and nurtured.

Yet time and again, under the leadership of chief justices Rehnquist and Roberts, the Court has disparaged the context-sensitive method of interpretation we must use to explain this uncontroversial conclusion. While purporting to apply the "reasonable expectation of privacy" test, the Court has given it a grudging, artificial meaning. The Court will not permit the warrantless use of sophisticated technology to find out about activity *inside* a residence, even when the technology reveals only details that convey little or no personal information—such as the heat patterns disclosed by a thermal imaging device. Justice Antonin Scalia, writing for the Court, has declared that "in the home,...*all* details are intimate details."[10] And this, he said, remains true even when police acquire the information without physically entering the space. But the Court has repeatedly denied protection for personal activity and papers located *outside* a house, so long as the police actions do not amount to a trespass under old common-law rules. Without expressly repudiating *Katz*, the Court has in effect reinstated the eighteenth-century view that private information and private activity get little constitutional protection anywhere beyond a small inner sanctum— the four walls of the home.

A series of "beeper" cases signaled the return to this outmoded conception of the Fourth Amendment. Unsurprisingly, the Court held that secretly placing an electronic signaling device inside a residence, in order to track movements there, qualifies as a "search" and therefore violates the Fourth Amendment in the absence of a search warrant.[11] But the Court reached the opposite conclusion when government agents were able to track a suspect's movements *outside* the home without disturbing any of his property. (They had simply planted a beeper inside a container that they delivered to him and then tracked as he drove away with it.) Of course, a person's movements on the street were not considered private in the eighteenth century. And even today, what a person does outdoors can be observed by anyone standing nearby. Seizing on these facts, and ignoring the capacity of electronic tracking to produce a detailed picture that was unimaginable in the eighteenth century, the Rehnquist Court held that use of a beeper to locate and track a suspect outdoors (in other words, *searching* for him) is not a "search" in the *constitutional* sense.[12]

The contemporary Court has also stripped away constitutional protection from information that citizens never expose to the general public at all. In a 1976 case, federal agents ordered bank officers to turn over all records pertaining to a depositor's checking and savings accounts. Of course, the records fell squarely within the terms of the Fourth Amendment; they were "papers" of the traditional sort. And the bank, like most financial intermediaries, had pledged to keep them confidential. Yet the Burger Court exploited the flexible "expectations" test to *reduce* the citizen's privacy protection. It held that a bank customer has no "reasonable expectation of privacy" because he "voluntarily" gives the information to the bank and therefore "takes the risk" that bank employees will provide it to the government—even when the government forces them to do so.[13]

Three years later the Court used the same artificial assumption of voluntary choice to deny protection against a sophisticated surveillance technology. The Court held that agents needed no warrant to tap into telephone wires and attach a "pen register," a device that reveals the numbers an individual dials. The Court said that callers assumed this risk because they "voluntarily conveyed [the] information to the telephone company and 'exposed' that information to its equipment."[14]

Continuing down this path, the Court has even permitted unregulated high-tech surveillance of parts of the home itself, so long as the area observed lies outside its four walls. In a California case, officers who had no warrant or probable cause hired a small airplane and flew over a private residence at an altitude of one thousand feet in order to determine whether the owner was growing marijuana in his backyard. The space surrounding a residence (called the "curtilage" at common law) has always been considered a protected part of the home, and there is no doubt that the officers would have needed a warrant to climb over a fence and physically enter the yard. But the Rehnquist Court held that the owner had no "reasonable expectation" of protection from aerial surveillance because the information police had gathered was exposed to any traveler on a commercial flight who happened to use high-powered binoculars to look down while passing overhead.[15]

The Court likewise held there was no "search" when officers used a helicopter flying at four hundred feet to look through a glass roof into a greenhouse attached to a private residence. The Court said that because members of the general public could travel through the same airspace and observe activity in the greenhouse (provided they could afford to rent a helicopter and hire a pilot), there was no intrusion on "reasonable expectations," and police were therefore free to gather the information without judicial oversight.[16]

These decisions about beepers, bank records, overflights, and countless surveillance tactics in between, make protection of informational privacy—one of the Fourth Amendment's central goals— simply impossible to achieve in the modern world. Yet the Court's reasoning is not mysterious. The information at stake is not truly private, the Court has said, because the facts are *already exposed*, and the citizen has *chosen* to expose them. The citizen has therefore *assumed the risk* that others will notice the information.

Yet if this reasoning is sound, warrantless surveillance should have been upheld in *Katz* itself. Katz had placed his call from a public location, he had "chosen" to do so, and the courts could have said he "assumed the risk" that government agents would listen in. But as we have seen, the justices cannot decide Fourth Amendment questions by asking whether someone has assumed a risk, because the risks we assume are in large part a function of the law itself. It is the law—in other words, the Court's understanding of the Fourth Amendment—that determines which risks the government can require us to assume.

The question we must ask is whether the goal of the Fourth Amendment—a world where citizens have a reasonable opportunity to lead private lives, free from indiscriminate government spying— is defeated by permitting a particular type of unregulated surveillance. The warrantless eavesdropping in *Katz* did not involve any physical trespass, and it did not expose anything happening in the home. It nonetheless violated the Fourth Amendment because it gave the government access to personal information that the citizen has no practical way to shield from that sort of spying.

True, Katz did not *have to* use the telephone. He could have arranged to meet his friend face-to-face at his home. But to put the citizen to this choice—to deny protection to interactions that are indispensable in modern life—would, as the *Katz* Court recognized, "ignore the vital role that the public telephone has come to play in private communication."[17] Like "X-ray vision" that can penetrate opaque walls and drawn curtains, the electronic microphone trumps all realistically available means for shielding precious details of personal life from unwelcome eyes and ears.

Of course, "X-ray vision" devices are constitutionally allowable under some circumstances—metal detectors at airports, for example. But no one doubts that they are "searches" governed by the Fourth Amendment. We now take them for granted and assume they are permissible, but that conclusion is correct only because these screening programs are executed in a manner that courts have found to be reasonable. The electronic eavesdropping in the *Katz* case likewise would have been lawful if authorized by a warrant. But because the slap mike made it impossible for Katz to shield his phone conversation, surveillance of this type cannot be indiscriminate and unregulated. To conclude otherwise would demolish our ability to claim the sheltered space that the Framers sought to preserve against government encroachment.

SHARED INFORMATION

The Supreme Court's crabbed conception of "reasonable expectations" has emerged from situations where citizens allowed details of their personal lives to escape beyond the protective walls of a home or phone booth. Our movements on the street are visible to motorists and pedestrians, activity in our backyards is (theoretically) visible to air travelers, and our checking accounts are visible to clerks at the bank. In these situations, the Court's "third-party doctrine" declares that individuals are not entitled to protection from government spying, because they "choose" to reveal personal information to others.

This reasoning is inexcusably formalistic. As Justice Lewis Powell noted when he dissented in the California overflight case, there is no conceivable risk that ordinary commercial air passengers will pay attention to what an individual is doing in a backyard thousands of feet below them. The police had used expensive equipment to see into a fenced area not visible to ordinary passersby, just as federal agents had used sophisticated electronics to eavesdrop on a phone booth conversation no one else could overhear. If anything, aerial surveillance is far more intrusive than the slap mike used in the *Katz* case, because low-level overflights allow authorities to monitor behavior in a part of the home itself, an area traditionally devoted to intimate activity. Yet the Court allowed a purely theoretical risk to trigger exposure to a much larger and much more disturbing risk—the prospect of purposeful spying by unchecked law enforcement officers, precisely the risk that the Fourth Amendment is intended to mitigate.

Decisions like these are defensible only if a form of personal privacy treasured for centuries is now less important than enabling police to spot homegrown marijuana without having to bother with probable cause. Unregulated overflights give the police access to personal activity—lawful as well as illicit—that otherwise would remain completely secret.

The cases involving telephone call records (the "pen register") are a bit different because the individual targeted by those searches really *has* shared the relevant details (the phone numbers he calls) by transmitting them to his telecom provider. But to treat information conveyed to a trusted intermediary, under promise of confidentiality, as if it had been posted on a public billboard is to make nonsense of the Fourth Amendment.

Of course, employees occasionally misuse information, and breaches of confidentiality sometimes occur. But the Court has taken this unavoidable risk of wrongdoing as a basis for allowing something that is entirely avoidable and far more alarming—the possibility of unrestricted, intentional scrutiny by government investigators. If the Court's reasoning were sound, the justices could just as easily hold that the risk of burglary defeats a property owner's expectation of privacy and renders warrantless searches of the home permissible as well. The Court's approach to "assumption of risk" permits virtually *non-existent* risks (observation by commercial air travelers) and risks of *unlawful* conduct (breach of confidentiality by intermediaries) to defeat any expectation of protection from unconstrained government spying.

To be sure, recording only the phone numbers dialed is less intrusive than recording the *content* of a conversation. But the Court's pen register decision (*Smith v. Maryland,* 1979) did not depend on whether the details obtained were important. To explain why the caller's privacy expectation was not "reasonable," the Court emphasized that he had "voluntarily" chosen to expose the information.[18] Because the linchpin is this supposedly voluntary choice, the Court could hold in *Miller v. United States* (1976) that highly personal financial records confidentially entrusted to a bank deserve no constitutional safeguards either.[19]

This approach leaves the lion's share of all contemporary communication—email, social networking (even on nonpublic sites), phone calls by digital transmission, and the like—with no Fourth Amendment shield.* When the "third-party doctrine" first became prominent (in the 1970s), communication still consisted primarily of

---

* Congress has filled part of this gap. Telephone calling records, email, and some other forms of communication have statutory protection under certain circumstances. But those safeguards are much weaker than the ones mandated where the Fourth Amendment governs. When information is protected only by statute, prosecutors often have access to it without probable cause, and the remedies for failure to respect statutory requirements are limited.

hard-copy correspondence through the Postal Service and conversations that occurred in person or by telephone. Whatever the theoretical reach of its reasoning, the *Smith* decision (denying Fourth Amendment protection against pen registers) represented a limited incursion on privacy, because the *content* of personal communication was not put in jeopardy.

Yet today email, Twitter, and the like have gone far toward displacing first-class mail and the telephone as citizens' primary means of communication. Video-conferencing has not wholly replaced the face-to-face meeting (yet), but it represents a step in that direction, and sometimes it relies on digital information processed on a server before and during transmission. If the technical structure of these devices can defeat Fourth Amendment protection, we will retain little ability to shield our ideas and our associations from the penetrating gaze of government agencies.

To be sure, the routing information in our email is the functional equivalent of the telephone numbers that current Fourth Amendment law does not protect. But the *content* of our email is the functional equivalent of the content of a phone conversation. On any sensible approach to communications privacy, email content and telephone content should have identical protection. Yet if the Court continues to focus on a citizen's "voluntary" decision to communicate through an intermediary, the body of an email message "exposed" to an Internet service provider (ISP) will fall into the same legal category as phone numbers transmitted to the telecom company or financial records conveyed confidentially to a bank.

A few lower courts have sought to avoid this conclusion. One recent appellate decision recognizes that the thirty-year-old formula designed for "pen register" technology cannot be extended blindly and that modern network communication deserves constitutional protection.[20] But if the Supreme Court adheres to the artificial logic of its third-party doctrine, email, phone conversations transmitted digitally, and many other intimate communications will receive no Fourth Amendment safeguards, because messages sent through network servers do not remain completely secret.

The problem here is not just that a once-valid constitutional principle now has awkward implications. The notion that shared information should have no Fourth Amendment protection has *always* been untenable, because privacy has never been equated with mere secrecy. It is something much more important: the *right to control* knowledge about our personal lives, the right to decide how much information gets revealed to whom and for which purposes.

Only a hermit can lay claim to complete secrecy. For anyone who wishes to inhabit the world, daily life inevitably involves personal associations and the information we exchange within them. Relationships give meaning to our lives and define a large part of who we are. To insist that information is private only when it remains completely secret is preposterous. Indeed, personal information often becomes *more* valuable when we share it confidentially with chosen associates who help us pursue common projects. As Judge Richard Posner puts it, "productive independent thinking almost always requires bouncing ideas off other people."[21] Though shared, the information remains *private* until we relinquish control and expose it to the public.

In contemporary experience, where social networks have pervasive importance, this reality is especially clear. But even in the eighteenth century, the claim that the right to privacy requires complete secrecy would have been incomprehensible. The colonists who conferred with friends while planning the American revolution did not think that by sharing confidential information they had lost their right to exclude strangers. They did not think that by sending a message to their doctor, banker, or collaborator they had given the Crown unregulated power to seize it. Justice Scalia explains this point clearly: "It is privacy that is protected by the Fourth

Amendment, not solitude. A man enjoys Fourth Amendment protection in his home, for example, though his wife and children have the run of the place—and, indeed, even though his landlord has the right to conduct unannounced inspections at any time."[22] The notion of granting Fourth Amendment protection only when information is completely secret would have been incoherent, even in the simple, technology-free world of 1791.

Personal details that we make available *to the general public* are different, of course. Usually we can shelter them if we wish. We cannot—and should not—expect to retain control over information that we display in a living room window or post on websites open to all. But when the Court says that a telephone user "chooses" to reveal his calling patterns to his telecom company, it implies that the customer can communicate in some other way, and that is simply not true. To reason in this manner is to do precisely what the Court in *Katz* condemned, ignoring the vital role the telephone has come to play in modern life. Once we acknowledge that electronic media have become essential for maintaining personal relationships, the decision to use them is not "voluntary," and those who send email have not in any meaningful sense "chosen" to assume the risk of government spying.

The same point applies to our bank accounts and to the gardens behind our homes. People sometimes run risks they can reasonably avoid, and if they do, they have no claim to Fourth Amendment protection—for example, if they leave a diary on a park bench or grow marijuana in a yard easily seen by neighbors. But there is no such choice when we use a bank account or spend time on a patio protected by a dense hedge. The Court's claim that we expose information in these places "voluntarily" is equivalent to an announcement that Americans who want to shield their personal beliefs and associations need only opt to make all their purchases in cash, conduct all confidential communications face-to-face (after resigning themselves to interact only with friends and family who live nearby), and either carry out their personal activities indoors or else build an opaque dome over their backyards.

This is obvious nonsense. The option these rulings leave us is, in effect, the option to withdraw from normal community life. That cannot have been the price the Framers expected us to pay for retaining any claim to privacy. They most assuredly did not consider personal friendship and social engagement to be incompatible with a right to prevent indiscriminate government spying. The Fourth Amendment was designed to nurture and support civic life, not to provide an alternative to it.

One way to clarify intuitions about "third-party disclosure" is to focus not on *voluntary choice* (the Court's emphasis) but instead on *inescapable risk*. The Court should have acknowledged from the outset that we cannot avoid relying on intermediaries like banks and telecom providers. In reality, there is no meaningful alternative. Yet even when we disclose personal matters only for a limited purpose, some of our ability to control access to the information is inevitably lost, whether we like it or not. Employees we have never met will be handling our personal accounts, and they may gossip indiscreetly or use what they see for improper purposes.

Disclosure to others in early America was different. Citizens typically shared personal information only within a small circle of trusted friends and acquaintances. They could judge for themselves the reliability of associates in whom they confided. Although they faced a risk that a friend might spread gossip or turn to the police, their privacy remained intact so long as the friend remained loyal, and they did not lose their right to exclude unwanted strangers. When an eighteenth-century colonist invited a neighbor into his home and permitted her to observe his intimate surroundings, he took a risk that the neighbor would violate his trust. But his act of hospitality certainly did not give *the government* the power to enter his home at any time against his will.

The same point applies to Katz's phone conversation. The risk that his statements would be disclosed depended on the trustworthiness of the person he called, and that risk was largely under his control. The Court's claim that the Fourth Amendment gives no right to block unregulated government scrutiny of shared information cannot possibly apply to matters revealed only within a limited circle of personal acquaintances.

If the justices sensed some difference between Katz, who shared a conversation with one associate, and Miller, who shared financial records with his bank, their intuition may have reflected this difference in the depth and intimacy of the two relationships. When private material is entrusted to impersonal institutions, unknown agents and employees gain access to it. Weighing and controlling the risks of misuse becomes difficult.

But not impossible. An Internet user can configure her browser settings to a variety of privacy levels. She can choose an ISP committed to confidentiality rather than one that shares customer data freely with its advertisers. Banks, hospitals, ISPs, and other indispensable institutions tout their dedication to client privacy and compete for business on that basis. When Google recently launched the social networking site Google+, it sought to challenge the dominant position of Facebook by "decid[ing] to make privacy the No. 1 feature of its new service."[23] These intermediaries also have an incentive to root out unreliable employees, so that information entrusted to them is used only as intended.

In an increasingly impersonal world, some service providers take special pains to personalize their customer relationships, an approach that many clients value. The Supreme Court's view that information conveyed to a third party is inevitably at risk of misuse is far too sweeping at a time when service providers, adapting to market pressure and to their own expanding responsibilities, have become quite sensitive to privacy concerns. But even in Katz's day, telephone company personnel had the right to listen in on customers' calls under limited circumstances. That fact did not eliminate the telephone user's reasonable expectation to be protected from unrestricted government eavesdropping. The appropriate conclusion here is simple: Fourth Amendment safeguards should apply whenever citizens convey personal information to a trusted third party under promise of confidentiality.

Because the permissive third-party doctrine has been embedded in law enforcement practice for at least thirty years, judges will certainly want to consider the practical effects of overturning it. But in the case of documents and records held by intermediaries, any governmental need to avoid Fourth Amendment oversight is *exceptionally weak*. An ordinary search typically intrudes on someone suspected of wrongdoing and seeks incriminating evidence that the target wants to conceal. Protection of privacy in that context must be weighed against legitimate law enforcement imperatives because the search must be executed without warning and with no opportunity for the suspect to interfere. There is seldom any such imperative in the case of evidence held by banks, HMOs, and telecom providers: A conventional subpoena to the third-party institution will suffice to afford access to the records, and the individual concerned can easily be given a chance to object in court, with no risk that incriminating information will be destroyed in the meantime. Any need for secrecy, speed, or surprise would be unusual and can be addressed through normal Fourth Amendment exceptions for exigency and special circumstances. There is no justification for leaving this entire domain of personal information exposed to unlimited fishing expeditions with no oversight at all.

In short, *Fourth Amendment safeguards should apply whenever individuals convey personal information to a service provider or other intermediate institution under promise of confidentiality.*

DATA MINING

Data mining poses the problem in even starker form. When we buy a book, rent a movie, order from a restaurant, or check into a motel, these everyday transactions typically carry no promise of confidentiality. They are in "plain view," just like movements on the street. But usually no single transaction means much by itself, just as crossing a particular intersection at a particular time is seldom revealing in itself. For practical purposes, there is virtually no risk that a casual observer will infer anything at all about our private lives. But officials conducting focused investigations are not merely casual observers. The threats to our personal security change completely when government officials, aided by modern technology, acquire the capacity to scour mountains of "plain view" information lodged at scores of unrelated sites. Software that aggregates and analyzes countless megabytes of disparate detail can identify patterns and point a law enforcement officer toward individuals who meet predetermined criteria—whether for drug use, bribery, "radical" politics, patronizing of prostitutes, or any other subject that interests the investigator.

Until recently, nearly all courts assumed that the "beeper" cases and other "plain view" decisions rule out any possibility of Fourth Amendment protection against technologies that allow the government to infer intensely personal details by mining data banks and then aggregating and analyzing the masses of information they contain. Yet the capacity of these tools to penetrate our private lives was unimaginable in the eighteenth or even in the mid-twentieth century. Like unrestricted wiretapping, the new data-mining technologies have the potential to obliterate large segments of the zone of privacy that the Fourth Amendment exists to protect.

Commercial data mining has some of the same potential—an argument for permitting police to do the same thing. But there are fundamental differences. Most basically, we routinely deny government the power to pursue actions that are freely available to individuals. Private citizens are free to promote a specific religion, support a particular political party, and use their personal capabilities in many ways of their own choosing. Indeed, one central purpose of our Constitution is to protect *individual* freedom, while restraining the powers of *government*. And for good reason. The extraordinary resources available to the government give it unique power and unique potential to threaten the liberty and autonomy of individuals. A preference for leaving activity in the private sector unregulated (if possible) is an axiom of our political system; a preference for unchecked *government* power is the antithesis of our Bill of Rights.

In matters involving personal information, the unique dangers of government power raise particularly concrete concerns. Federal agencies such as the National Security Agency can deploy computer capability and analytic sophistication that dwarf anything available in the private sector. Yet under the Supreme Court's current approach, once an ordinary citizen can theoretically access various tidbits of information, the government can use any technology, no matter how elaborate and expensive, to aggregate and analyze them.

Government data mining also poses distinctive risks of abuse. Commercial data collection and analysis subjects us almost daily to unwelcome, machine-generated email and phone calls; we are offered products and services we have no desire to buy. This is a nuisance, but the harm is trivial. When commercial data analysis improperly taints a consumer's credit rating, the injury is more serious. But lenders have an incentive to weed out inaccurate reports, and borrowers are increasingly afforded an opportunity to correct them. The dangers are entirely different when personal information becomes available to the government, with its vast power over the lives of individuals. Investigators seeking to prevent public awareness of controversial government actions can use data-mining software to ascertain a journalist's confidential sources. Data mining gives the government access to a citizen's political and religious beliefs, personal associations, sexual interests, or other matters that can expose the individual to political intimidation, blackmail, or selective prosecution for trivial infractions.

Supreme Court doctrines rooted in the simpler world of the 1970s and 1980s seem to preclude any Fourth Amendment protection against such dangers. The Court's most recent encounter with these problems hints at some flexibility but also indicates much confusion and uncertainty about the way forward.

District of Columbia police, acting without a valid warrant, attached a GPS tracking device to the car of a drug suspect, Antoine Jones, and used it to record his whereabouts, twenty-four hours a day, for four weeks. At any moment during that period, Jones's location and movements in his car were exposed to the general public, and for this reason several appellate courts had held that GPS tracking of this sort does not intrude on a reasonable expectation of privacy. But in the D.C. case, the Supreme Court held otherwise (*United States v. Jones*, 2012). A majority of five justices, in an opinion by Justice Antonin Scalia, said the decisive point was that the police, by placing the GPS device on the underside of the suspect's car, had touched the vehicle without permission and thus had committed a trespass under ancient common-law rules.[24] All the information acquired as a result was therefore inadmissible.

What this outcome means for the future of the Fourth Amendment is unclear, to say the least. Although the Court upheld Jones's constitutional claim, the decision is far from reassuring. By tying its conclusion to a legal fine point (the common-law trespass), the Court's majority focused exclusively on an eighteenth-century technicality that was irrelevant to the only serious problem presented in the case.

The real concern in *Jones*, as all the Justices knew, was that a GPS, regardless of how it may be attached, creates a precise, detailed, permanent record of a person's movements—one that police can preserve and mine for information at their convenience for years into the future. Intensely personal matters are brought easily within the government's reach: "trips to the psychiatrist, the plastic surgeon, the abortion clinic, the AIDS treatment center, the strip club, the criminal defense attorney, the by-the-hour motel, the union meeting, the mosque, synagogue or church, the gay bar and on and on."[25] Although ordinary eye-contact surveillance was always able to pick up details like these, finite law enforcement resources ensured that in practice, the risk of exposure to such surveillance was minimal. Police inevitably had to set priorities; they could rarely if ever subject a citizen to prolonged covert visual surveillance. All this changes when police can, at minimal cost, learn about every potentially telling personal trip made by virtually everyone.

And that threat to privacy is only the beginning, because GPS surveillance can expose a great deal more. Even when a particular trip tells the police nothing by itself, the digital record allows the government to aggregate and analyze many individually innocuous details. Patterns of travel, repeated trips to a particular location, and the time spent there disclose far more than any casual observer—or even a large team of trained detectives—could possibly learn without high-tech assistance.

The outcome in *Jones* seems to offer a shield against these possibilities. But that appearance is deceiving because the constitutional violation, in the Court's eyes, rests on a point that is preposterously artificial. After all, the tracking device caused no damage to the vehicle and left Jones's possession of his property completely undisturbed; indeed such devices typically weigh no more than 2 ounces and are no bigger than a credit card. By basing the result on this minute detail, Justice Scalia resurrected the unworkable and distracting distinctions between slap mikes and spike mikes that the Court was impelled to abandon fifty years ago. As Justice Douglas noted at that time, "the depth of the penetration...is not the measure of the injury" (see page 118).

An even greater concern is that the protections of the old common-law trespass doctrine simply are not very much help. Many cars now have tracking devices installed by the manufacturer, so that the vehicle can be located in the event of theft. The installation occurs at the factory before delivery to the customer (thus no common-law trespass), and if police activate the device electronically, there is still no trespass—unless the Court compounds the artificiality of *Jones* by saying that eighteenth-century rules are violated when the activation signal (an electronic wave or particle) makes contact with the car. And regardless of how that issue is resolved, other methods of locational tracking are just around the corner or already here. Because wireless cell phones and "smart phones" communicate through a number of different towers at known locations, telecom company records can provide a trace of the user's movements whenever the phone was turned on, and this locational data is obtained without any sort of trespass because it is typically produced by *receiving* signals from the phone. The majority's approach in *Jones* offers virtually no defense against the government's ability to exploit the intrusive potential of technologies like these.

In an important concurring opinion that seems likely to influence future decisions, Justice Samuel Alito, joined by three other justices, agreed that Jones had been the victim of an unconstitutional search, but he emphatically rejected the trespass-based analysis of the majority. Justice Alito properly recognized that the police tactics were unacceptable because of their interference with *privacy*, not property. The technical trespass, he stressed, "can have no constitutional significance."[26] The justices who joined the

Alito concurrence apparently are ready to hold warrantless long-term tracking unconstitutional, regardless of how the locational data are collected.

Unfortunately, Justice Alito's approach contains grave limitations of its own. Although he found the four-week surveillance of Jones intolerable, he concluded that "relatively short-term" monitoring *is* permissible without a warrant. He gave no hint as to the permissible duration of "short-term" tracking, and he suggested that even very long-term monitoring might be acceptable when police are investigating "extraordinary offenses."[27]

These permissive conclusions flowed, for Justice Alito, from his belief that Americans have come to expect these police surveillance practices. But that expectation, of course, is partly a product of the Court's own opinions—for example, its questionable thirty-year-old decisions that uphold short-term beeper monitoring. And Justice Alito himself recognized that in a world of rapidly developing technology, public attitudes can change dramatically. This puts his constitutional framework on a foundation of sand. And he also suggested that when "new technology [provides] increased convenience or security at the expense of privacy,... people may find the tradeoff worthwhile."[28] Thus, the four justices who endorse this approach apparently conclude that if people are willing to accept tracking technology for their own use and for improved telecom service, they will necessarily lose any right to shield the locational data from unconstrained spying by government agencies. And in a final twist, Justice Alito declared that the necessary boundaries and safeguards might best be left to Congress: "A legislative body is well situated to gauge changing public attitudes, to draw detailed lines, and to balance privacy and public safety in a comprehensive way."[29]

We have seen this viewpoint—and its flaws—throughout this chapter. In contemporary life, we must inevitably rely on service providers and entrust them with personal information. The risk that their employees may, on rare occasions, misbehave by disclosing confidential facts or by snooping without authorization is in no way comparable to the exposure we face if the government can *compel* these organizations to turn over revealing personal facts. And even when bits of information about us are in theory accessible to any member of the public (like individual details concerning our movements during a single day), the chance that any stranger will pay enough attention to learn anything significant is negligible. In contrast, government officials intent on spying, and aided by powerful technology, can learn a great deal very quickly.

Against these dangers, the prospect of legislation affords little comfort. Even when a majority of citizens are sufficiently aroused to demand congressional action, their voices usually cannot compete with the Justice Department's ability (backed by the presidential veto power) to make law enforcement convenience the top priority in the legislative process. When the Court refused to require Fourth Amendment safeguards for pen-register surveillance of telephone call numbers, Congress responded by seeking to enact protective legislation, but the resulting statute merely requires the FBI to certify that the information sought is "relevant to an ongoing criminal investigation."[30] In other words, the government only needs to file a self-certification that it is not acting in bad faith. Oversight cannot get much weaker than that.

Apart from this difficulty, however, is a more basic point. The major aim of the Fourth Amendment—unquestionably—is not to bolster majority rule but to afford shelter to political, religious, and ideological minorities. It would surely astonish the Framers—not to mention those who feel targeted for surveillance today (observant Muslims, for example)—to discover that the Fourth Amendment affords no protection against spying tactics considered tolerable in the eyes of mainstream public opinion.

Only Justice Sonia Sotomayor appreciated these dangers. In a separate opinion, she agreed that the government tactics in *Jones* were unconstitutional, but she refused to limit her concern to physical intrusions or to surveillance lasting weeks at a time. She stressed the wealth of personal detail that even brief locational tracking can expose and noted that similar dangers arise when the government is allowed unrestricted access to the voluminous personal data we entrust to third parties. As Justice Sotomayor rightly warned, "awareness that the Government may be watching chills associational and expressive freedoms" and is "susceptible to abuse."[31] Unfortunately, no other Justice joined this clear statement of what the Fourth Amendment should mean in the twenty-first century.

No one suggests that government data mining should be prohibited altogether. It can prevent great harm and can help catch dangerous wrongdoers. As always, the point of the Fourth Amendment is only to assure that invasive methods of investigation are subject to oversight. The upshot is straightforward: *If a technology that is not widely available overrides all realistically available options for shielding personal activities or associations from government spying, its use must be considered a "search" subject to Fourth Amendment safeguards.*

When the Framers of our Constitution established a zone of security for our "persons, houses, papers, and effects," their goal was not just to guard the tangible value of those forms of property. Indeed, they made separate provision (in the Fifth Amendment) for protecting private property from government taking without due process and just compensation. The aim of the Fourth Amendment is different—the preservation of a vibrant society that respects the freedom and autonomy of each individual. To maintain and nurture such a society, the Framers guaranteed our capacity to carve out a sheltered space in which we can try out new thoughts, explore new relationships, and develop our abilities, free from an all-seeing government eye that stifles creativity and independence.

For the Framers, the home represented not just a claim on a piece of real estate but a refuge, a haven shielded from the nosiness, prurience, and hostility of strangers. What made that haven indispensable, as Pitt eloquently declared in 1765, was not the physical shelter it might (or might not) provide from wind and rain but its capacity to foster peace of mind by preventing the unwanted scrutiny of government investigators (chapter 2). As the world changes rapidly around us, human nature has not changed, and that sheltered space remains as important as ever for healthy, flourishing individuals in a healthy, flourishing democracy.

Because the new technologies make this need for refuge more essential than ever, they pose a twofold challenge. We must recognize the continuing importance of those sheltered spaces. And we must insist that our courts restore the Fourth Amendment to its intended position as a mechanism for preserving those spaces in the face of unprecedented technological, social, and political pressures.

CHAPTER SEVEN

The National Security Challenge

If the Court does not temper its doctrinaire logic with a little practical wisdom, it will convert the constitutional Bill of Rights into a suicide pact.

—JUSTICE ROBERT H. JACKSON (1949)

. . .

A state of war is not a blank check for the President when it comes to the rights of the Nation's citizens.

—JUSTICE SANDRA DAY O'CONNOR (2004)

. . .

Though the investigative duty of the executive may be stronger in [national security] cases, so also is there greater jeopardy to constitutionally protected speech.... History abundantly documents the tendency of Government—however benevolent and benign its motives—to view with suspicion those who most fervently dispute its policies. Fourth Amendment protections become the more necessary when the targets of official surveillance may be those suspected of unorthodoxy.... The price of lawful public dissent must not be a dread of subjection to an unchecked surveillance power.

—JUSTICE LEWIS POWELL (1972)

. . .

WITH SEPTEMBER 11, 2001, fresh in memory and additional attacks, perhaps even more devastating, still impossible to rule out, many see traditional Fourth Amendment strictures as luxuries intended for less dangerous times. Yet the Framers and their successors were thoroughly familiar with insurrection, war, and other existential threats to democratic government.

Only a few years after the Revolutionary War, farmers in Massachusetts organized a private army to attack the newly independent state government (Shay's Rebellion). President George Washington faced an armed uprising in western Pennsylvania (the Whiskey Rebellion), and the British burned our nation's new capital to the ground during the War of 1812. The Civil War brought destruction to vast stretches of our landscape, and rebels far behind the battle lines spied and committed sabotage. In Maryland, Confederate sympathizers disrupted the transit points carrying troops and supplies to defend the capital. At war's end, the president himself was assassinated, not by a lone madman but by plotters supported by a network of citizens disloyal to the Union. After World War I and the Russian Revolution, after Pearl Harbor, and again during the Cold War, the country was once more preoccupied by fear that treacherous individuals, hiding in our midst, dangerous and hard to identify, threatened our security and the very foundations of our democracy.

In all these periods, civil liberties came under assault, often by well-meaning citizens convinced they were living through a period of unique danger. Each time, from the Sedition Act of 1798 through the Red Scare of the 1920s, the internments of Japanese Americans in 1942–44, and the communist witch hunts of the 1950s, Americans came to regret their overly fearful responses, realizing that civil liberties had been sacrificed needlessly and at great cost.[1]

Future generations may look back on the first decades of the twenty-first century with similar remorse and embarrassment. Yet, even knowing that Americans overreacted in previous emergencies, we should also acknowledge distinctive features of the present threat. Easily concealed weapons can now inflict devastating loss of life and economic injury running to the billions of dollars in a single successful attack. Conventional methods of deterring potential offenders and punishing those who aren't deterred—the prospect of arrests on probable cause, followed by indictments, criminal trials, convictions (when warranted), and imprisonment—obviously offer no defense against the suicide bomber who is willing to die for his cause. The protective strategies of conventional warfare—deterrence and military retaliation against state actors—are likewise inadequate, if not irrelevant.

A majority of Americans seem to assume that traditional Fourth Amendment safeguards must be relaxed, at least to some extent, in order to confront this threat and provide an extra margin of safety. Many who treasure the Bill of Rights see the sacrifice of some privacy as a small price to pay for preventing a catastrophic attack. Either they assume that constitutional rights must give way in an "emergency," or they assume that the rights themselves expand or contract, accordion-like, as countervailing security needs fluctuate.

That intuition has led Americans to accept a host of new laws weakening traditional constraints on the executive. The nation has also tolerated law enforcement actions that disregard limits supposedly still in force. Existing Fourth Amendment requirements, already weakened by decades of Supreme Court precedent, have come under further attack. Statutory remedies for flaws in pre-9/11 Supreme Court precedent never had the constitutional status they deserve, and many of them have been rolled back under the pressures of the moment. When it comes to international terrorism, most people seem to assume that individuals like themselves will not come under suspicion. And even if they think that their own privacy may be affected, in matters of national security they prefer not to take chances. As a result, restraints have eroded across the entire spectrum of search-and-seizure powers.

DETENTION WITHOUT CHARGE

None of those restraints is more fundamental than the rule prohibiting detention on the unilateral say-so of the executive. There must be a charge, and the person seized must have an opportunity for speedy judicial review. Nearly eight hundred years ago in Magna Carta (1215), the cornerstone of English liberty, King John agreed that "no freeman shall be captured or imprisoned...except by the lawful judgment of his peers or by the law of the land." When later kings began to nullify that commitment by evasion and delay, the Habeas Corpus Act (1679) guaranteed *prompt* access to the courts. Our own Constitution prohibits suspension of the writ of habeas corpus, except by act of Congress, and even then, only "when in cases of War or Rebellion the public safety may require it." And to prevent the repetition of a scenario such as the shameful internment of Japanese Americans during World War II, Congress officially apologized for those actions and prohibited any detention of an American citizen except as authorized explicitly by statute.

Yet after 9/11, prior lessons were quickly forgotten. The most well-known example, of course, is Guantánamo, where hundreds of individuals claiming to be ordinary civilians were labeled "enemy combatants" and held for years before they had any access to the courts. Ordinary Fourth Amendment search-and-seizure rules do not apply when foreign nationals are arrested abroad,* but the basic principles of constitutional government underlying the Fourth Amendment—executive accountability and judicial review—do apply, and these principles were disregarded for far too long. Many of the detainees were held for more than six years before the Supreme Court finally ruled that U.S. courts could hear their habeas corpus petitions.[2]

Just as troublesome are many of the actions taken within our own borders, where the Fourth Amendment applies directly. In the first two months following the 9/11 attacks, federal agents arrested and detained twelve hundred foreign nationals living in the United States, nearly all from the Middle East and South Asia. Most were never accused of a crime but were held only for violating administrative rules, such as overstaying a visa. By the end of November 2001, more than six hundred remained in custody.[3]

The initial arrests were not necessarily illegal, but the detainees then suffered grave violations of their Fourth Amendment rights. Though they faced only civil immigration charges, 548 individuals were designated as "special interest" cases because of suspected links to terrorism, often on the basis of little more than their countries of origin. They were then held in strict secrecy, with no ability to retain counsel or communicate with the outside world. Their hearings were held behind closed doors, giving them little opportunity to challenge the government's accusations.[4]

---

* A few Guantánamo detainees were seized during combat in Afghanistan, a situation where the laws of war grant military forces broad detention powers. But most were arrested while living as civilians in cities around the world. Although our Fourth Amendment warrant requirement does not apply overseas, related American principles of due process and access to courts clearly apply, as the Supreme Court ultimately held.

Nearly all "special interest" detainees were ultimately cleared of terrorist ties and found guilty only of technical infractions, for example, taking a part-time job after entry on a tourist visa. But instead of releasing or deporting them, the Justice Department claimed that their breach of visa regulations exposed them to indefinite detention. Turning ordinary practice upside down, the administration treated their infractions as a basis to *prevent* them from leaving, and they were incarcerated for months without ever being informed of the real reasons they were being held. In a subsequent report, the inspector general of the Department of Justice found that large numbers of detainees had suffered abusive treatment and extended detention that was not justified by any legitimate national security concern.[5]

American citizens and foreign nationals living lawfully in the United States were not spared in these sweeps. José Padilla, a U.S. citizen born in Chicago, was arrested at Chicago's O'Hare International Airport, charged with being an "enemy combatant," and held incommunicado at a naval brig in Charleston, South Carolina, with no access to counsel, his family, or the courts. The U.S. courts took more than six years to signal their willingness to grant Padilla relief. At that point, the government withdrew its "enemy combatant" allegations and brought ordinary criminal charges, as it should have done all along. Padilla was ultimately convicted of serious crimes, but that outcome cannot excuse the flagrant disregard of Fourth Amendment principles involved in holding him for years in harsh conditions of confinement with no judicial review. In hundreds of other cases, citizens and lawful residents were held for excessive periods as "material witnesses." This legal device, intended only to preserve testimony, was used for preventive detention of suspects against whom the government lacked the evidence needed to bring criminal charges. Again, the Justice Department's inspector general found grave mistreatment of detainees and abuse of legal powers intended for other purposes.[6]

We can be thankful that none of these missteps matches the scale of the internments of Japanese Americans during World War II, and many of the overreactions have been scaled back. But misguided responses to terrorism have infected conventional search and surveillance methods as well. And in this instance the erosion of traditional constitutional safeguards is not only unwise but systematic and ongoing.

SNEAK-AND-PEEK SEARCHES

The Fourth Amendment permits unannounced searches when immediate notice to the property owner would defeat the purpose of the investigation. In what is called "sneak and peek," police enter while occupants are away, inspect the premises or install a surveillance device, and wait several days before informing the owner that the intrusion occurred (see chapter 3, pages 47–48).

Before September 11, 2001, sneak-and-peek searches were reserved for unusual circumstances and subjected to close judicial control. The Patriot Act (2001) expanded federal authority to make these delayed notice searches, even in routine domestic law enforcement investigations. In addition, and much more alarming, the Act authorized the FBI to conduct clandestine entries in "foreign intelligence" investigations without ever giving notice to the homeowner at all, even when the agents' primary purpose was to gather evidence for criminal prosecution of an American citizen.

Brandon Mayfield felt the full force of these powers. In March 2004, coordinated terror attacks on commuter trains in Madrid killed 191 persons and injured over sixteen hundred more. While helping Spanish police identify a fingerprint found with bomb-making material near the scene, the FBI determined that one of twenty possible matches belonged to Mayfield, a former American military officer who was living and practicing law in Portland, Oregon. When the FBI discovered that Mayfield was a convert to Islam, the agents felt sure they had their man.

FBI agents then launched a series of sneak-and-peek searches, examining Mayfield's files, tapping his phones, and planting listening devices in his law office and home. The searches were executed so carelessly that the Mayfield family become frightened, convinced they had been repeatedly burglarized. Even after Spanish police informed the U.S. government that Mayfield's prints did not match the originals in their possession, the FBI persisted in treating him as a prime suspect. They executed additional searches and seized countless records and materials, including even some of his children's homework. Next—and long after the Spanish police had exonerated Mayfield of any involvement—he was arrested, informed he was facing the death penalty, and held in custody as a "material witness" to the bombings. Justice Department and FBI leaks to the media fueled national and international headlines identifying Mayfield as a conspirator in the Madrid attacks. After he had been held incommunicado for two weeks, and only after the Spanish police announced publicly that they had arrested the Algerian man to whom the prints really belonged, did the FBI finally acknowledge its error and release Mayfield. Ultimately, the government agreed to pay him a substantial (though undisclosed) sum in damages.[7]

Mayfield's may be an isolated case of mistreatment—or he may be one of hundreds of Americans who have suffered from inexcusable sneak-and-peek operations. It is impossible to know how often the foreign intelligence sneak-and-peek is abused because nearly all details are highly classified. Of course, some secrecy is appropriate in investigations of this sort—no one suggests otherwise. What cannot be justified is the minimal degree of oversight and the lack of any opportunity for most citizens wrongfully searched to seek a remedy. Mayfield's highly publicized arrest at least allowed him to learn why his home had been broken into. In almost every other instance, foreign intelligence sneak-and-peeks never face the independent after-the-fact scrutiny that our Fourth Amendment tradition requires. And without some oversight mechanism to prevent misuse, clandestine searches squander investigative resources and infringe privacy unnecessarily. Paradoxically, such broad, unchecked powers usually do not even reduce the overall risk of a successful terrorist attack; as we will see in the course of this chapter, such powers actually tend to make us *less* safe.

THE PAPER TRAIL OF OUR PRIVATE LIVES

Because the Supreme Court's "third-party doctrine" unjustifiably withdraws most Fourth Amendment protection for personal information held for us by our banks, doctors, telecom companies, and other service providers (chapter 6), Americans have had to rely on statutory safeguards, and these are not only limited but subject to the changing winds of public opinion and perceived law enforcement needs. Nonetheless, for more than thirty years before 9/11, federal laws required the FBI to invoke a judicially supervised subpoena process to obtain most kinds of records. In foreign intelligence investigations, a simplified procedure was available, but only for the records of certain travel-related businesses. And even then, the FBI had to give a designated federal judge its reasons for believing that the records pertained to a foreign agent or a suspected international terrorist.[8]

After 9/11, with the FBI demanding greater freedom from oversight, Congress systematically weakened these safeguards. The Patriot Act made a streamlined approach available not just for business documents but for all papers and records held by third parties, including library circulation lists, the membership lists of religious organizations, and other personal material. And while eliminating previous limits on the kind of records available, Congress also watered down the requirements for invoking the simplified procedure. In foreign intelligence matters, the FBI can now get personal documents held under a promise of confidentiality merely by asserting that the documents are "relevant" to an authorized investigation. In other words, the FBI need do little more than give its word that it is not acting in bad faith.[9] The prerequisite is so banal that judicial oversight has become purely mechanical, a perfunctory rubber stamp.

While gutting oversight by the courts, the Patriot Act blocks accountability to Congress and the general public as well. Under its "gag order" provision, institutions that receive an FBI demand for documents cannot divulge to anyone the scope of the FBI intrusion into their confidential files. They can never reveal how much information or what kinds of information they were required to turn over. Of course, it is normal to expect that the target of an FBI investigation will be kept in the dark while the inquiry is under way. But the new "gag order" usually will prohibit any disclosure of the document demand for an unlimited period of time.

The immediate difficulty here is the direct interference with the service provider's freedom of speech.* But a major Fourth Amendment problem lies not far in the background, because the gag order shuts down the political checks that normally help prevent abuse of search and surveillance powers. Of course, the order prohibiting

---

* When lower courts held the gag order unconstitutional on First Amendment grounds, Congress gave the gag order recipient a process for asking a court to lift it. But that option remains difficult to invoke, and in any case most institutions subject to a gag order have little incentive to challenge it, because the privacy rights affected are not their own but only those of a small percentage of their customers.

disclosure serves the legitimate purpose of ensuring that suspects do not know when the FBI is on their trail, but it also ensures that no one else will know what the FBI is doing, not even in general terms or long after the fact.

Oversight cannot get much weaker than this, but the Patriot Act dilutes accountability still further through the device of the "national security letter" (NSL). Unlike the FBI's broad power to demand personal documents, the NSL can be used only to obtain financial records, telecom billing records, and credit agency reports. But this sort of information can be extraordinarily revealing. Our financial transactions, for example, provide a detailed picture of our private lives. Nonetheless, the records available through the NSL do not receive even the cursory judicial protection available for other documents. High-ranking FBI officials can issue NSLs on their own authority, and the institution holding the designated records must comply immediately. Thus, NSLs get no judicial scrutiny at all. And, like foreign intelligence document demands, they carry a broad gag order.

Before 9/11, NSLs, like other document demands, required the FBI to certify that the records pertained to a suspected terrorist or foreign agent. The Patriot Act replaced this weak requirement with an essentially meaningless one; the FBI is merely required to certify that the information is "sought for an authorized investigation." In addition, Congress multiplied several times over the range of information available through the NSL by including not only "financial" documents but also all records of "any other business... whose cash transactions have a high degree of usefulness in criminal, tax, or regulatory matters."[10]

The expanded NSL bypasses the courts altogether, and the FBI has not been slow to take advantage of it. Since 2001, the agency has issued forty to fifty thousand NSLs annually, a rate equivalent to more than one hundred NSL demands every day.[11] In 2010 alone,

NSL demands targeted more than fourteen thousand different Americans.[12]

The value of these personal documents to an FBI investigator is obvious. But the ability to obtain them without oversight should raise major Fourth Amendment concerns. Documents and records reveal intensely private information—travel patterns, medical histories, books we read, and the like. Personal records can be even more sensitive than the content of our phone conversations. At stake is the Fourth Amendment's most important objective, preserving for all citizens the ability to claim a private space in which they are free to explore new ideas and to claim some shelter from government scrutiny—what Brandeis called "the right to be let alone...the right most valued by civilized men."[13]

Political and religious liberty are implicated as well. Americans who follow a mainstream religion and take little interest in politics may not care whether the FBI knows what church they attend or what books they prefer. But a healthy democracy requires critics and dissenters. If the government can easily discover what everyone reads and with whom they associate, the ability to practice religion freely and to support unpopular causes is at grave risk.

These concerns need not lead us to block all FBI access to sensitive personal records. Fourth Amendment principles only require meaningful oversight—a simple precaution that the Patriot Act inexplicably eliminates. As investigatory powers increase, as they have since 9/11, the need for accountability becomes greater, not less. Only with independent judicial scrutiny can we ensure that document demands serve genuine needs and that legitimately acquired information is not used for improper purposes. Without oversight, government authority to acquire confidential private papers has enormous potential to chill the exercise of constitutional rights and stultify the freewheeling debate that is essential in a healthy democracy. As the 9/11 Commission's unanimous report warned, "This shift of power and authority to the government calls for an *enhanced* system of checks and balances to protect the precious liberties that are vital to our way of life."[14]

ELECTRONIC SURVEILLANCE

For many decades following World War II, presidents claimed a prerogative to conduct national security wiretapping without judicial approval. During the Vietnam War, however, the Supreme Court, in an opinion by Justice Lewis Powell, held that the president has no such authority, at least in connection with domestic threats. Even when "deemed necessary to protect the nation from attempts...to attack and subvert the existing structure of the Government," the Court said, such surveillance requires a warrant that meets Fourth Amendment standards—probable cause, particular description, and judicial oversight.[15] The Court did not rule on surveillance of foreign powers and their agents, but it signaled misgivings about unchecked executive authority even in that distinctive domain.

Soon after, Congress sought to put foreign intelligence activity on a sustainable footing. The Foreign Intelligence Surveillance Act of 1978 (FISA) established restrictions similar to the ordinary law enforcement regime discussed in chapter 6.[16] It requires a warrant based on probable cause, imposes strict time limits on surveillance, and mandates procedures to minimize the collection of unrelated information. But for foreign intelligence, FISA simplifies the warrant process, dilutes the required showing of probable cause, and reduces judicial oversight. And, of greatest importance, FISA stipulates that the targets of investigation, unlike individuals subjected to conventional law enforcement surveillance, normally need not be notified that they have been tapped. As a result, FISA operations face little review after the fact, and abuses are virtually impossible to detect.*

Because FISA can only be used against foreign powers or their agents, many people assume that the targets must be diplomats, spies, or international terrorists. In fact, FISA's reach is much broader. Any U.S. citizen can qualify as an "agent of a foreign power" if there are reasons to suspect her of possible national-security or foreign-policy crimes. Although that kind of suspicion would usually suffice for an ordinary criminal law warrant, the FISA alternative allows surveillance with more flexibility and *far* less oversight—in short, much more leeway than the government normally has even when it is investigating a domestic serial killer. This loophole—the FISA advantage in elasticity, secrecy, and reduced oversight—represents both its value and its danger.

The premise of FISA is that the government should have greater latitude when dealing with foreign threats, especially when its aim is *preventive*, rather than *punitive*. Like administrative searches that serve "special needs" (chapter 5), FISA searches are intended not to collect evidence for a criminal trial but to protect the United States from hostile nations and to prevent terror attacks before they can be launched. Until 9/11, therefore, the FBI was permitted to use FISA only when its *primary purpose* was to gather foreign intelligence, and not when it was pursuing a criminal investigation.

After 9/11, the Patriot Act eliminated the "primary purpose" requirement because it was seen as a hindrance to agency cooperation. Then Attorney General John Ashcroft took that change a step further by granting prosecutors the right to "direct or control" FISA

---

* For specific documentation of these problems and greater detail concerning the provisions of this complex statute, see Stephen J. Schulhofer, *Rethinking the Patriot Act*, 29–53 (New York: Century Foundation Press, 2005).

surveillance.[17] Like other responses to 9/11, the new surveillance measures augmented government powers much more than necessary. The difficulty of disentangling criminal investigations from preventive intelligence gathering provides a legitimate reason to relax the "primary purpose" requirement, but that step cannot justify permitting prosecutors to *take the lead* in operations that use FISA powers, rather than normal warrant procedures, to gather evidence for criminal cases. And instead of balancing increased powers with increased accountability, the post-9/11 changes made *reduced oversight* one of their principal objectives.[18]

Having requested and received this expansion of the relaxed FISA warrant process, the Bush administration decided to go much further. Immediately after 9/11, it established a secret program for *warrantless* surveillance of phone calls and email passing through American telecom facilities, whenever the sender or recipient of the message was located outside the United States. In that situation, contrary to the express requirements of FISA, the administration's secret regime bypassed the FISA court entirely. When news of this surveillance system surfaced in 2006, the administration offered confusing, inconsistent explanations of what it entailed and why it was thought necessary. A firestorm of criticism erupted, but support for the program was also strong, and those who disapproved focused primarily on procedural irregularities—the program's secrecy, lack of congressional involvement, and disregard of existing statutory requirements. These failings were important, to be sure, but a more fundamental concern should have been the *wisdom* and *constitutionality* of the program, with its underlying assumption that privacy and judicial oversight are obstacles to our security.

This time, Congress, to its credit, pushed back. After a long battle, it passed legislation barring much of what the Bush administration had been doing. The FISA Amendments Act of 2008 prohibits all foreign intelligence surveillance without a warrant if the target is inside the United States or if the person targeted, even outside the United States, is a U.S. citizen.[19] And for surveillance of foreign nationals outside the United States, the 2008 amendments give Congress and the courts an important oversight role. On the other side of the ledger, telecom companies involved in the original program were granted immunity from civil and criminal liability, even though their actions apparently had been in clear violation of FISA as it stood at the time.

Congress's action to restore FISA shows that as time passes, political leaders occasionally (if not promptly) can transcend national security panic and unthinking deference to officials who predictably seek ever wider powers. Nonetheless, the 2008 controversy cast FISA in a somewhat misleading light. Administration supporters portrayed FISA as exceedingly strict, a virtual straitjacket. On the opposing side of the debate, privacy advocates, by calling for adherence to the original FISA framework, in effect corroborated the assertion that its requirements had real teeth. So FISA emerged from the dispute with a new image as a meaningful bulwark of civil liberties. Yet that image is far from deserved, for FISA itself is needlessly porous. It fails to assure adequate oversight, and in permitting *prosecutors* to escape ordinary law enforcement requirements, it is especially objectionable. Robust congressional checks and timely notification to persons who have been wrongfully targeted are essential for assuring accountability, and these safeguards would threaten no legitimate need for flexibility or secrecy.

Like sneak-and-peek searches, NSLs, and powers to access personal documents, the post-9/11 FISA is an overbroad and unnecessary concession to security fears. For that reason, it represents not only an unsound policy choice but also an unjustifiable erosion of constitutionally mandated safeguards. Still, when the nation faces grave risks, the desire to "play it safe" is predictable and pervasive. The instinct to grant the government more power, even at some cost to traditional liberties, is an almost universal reaction to perilous circumstances. Yet the impulse to trade liberty for security is dangerously misinformed.

"BALANCING" LIBERTY AND SECURITY

Most Americans—experts and ordinary citizens alike—consider it self-evident that liberty and security are in conflict, and that efforts to enhance one invariably take a toll on the other. In the common metaphor, we must "balance" liberty against security. When external threats grow, protective measures must be strengthened, and this, most people believe, inevitably requires some sacrifice of our privacy.

For many, this notion of an inherent "trade-off" between liberty and national security is an obvious truth. Judge Richard Posner writes:

> civil liberties...are the point of balance between concerns for personal liberty and concerns for personal safety.... In times of danger, the weight of concerns for public safety increases relative to that of liberty concerns, and civil liberties are narrowed. In safer times, the balance shifts the other way and civil liberties are broadened.... Ideally, in the case of a right (for example the right to be free from unreasonable searches and seizures)...one would like to locate the point at which a slight expansion in the scope of the right would subtract more from public safety than it would add to personal liberty and a slight contraction would subtract more from personal liberty than it would add to public safety. That is the point of balance, and determines the optimal scope of the right. [We must] ask whether a particular security measure harms liberty more or less than it promotes safety.[20]

This way of thinking is deeply engrained. Liberals and conservatives typically assign different weights to various costs and benefits. But across the political spectrum, people largely accept that some trade-off between liberty and security is inevitable. Yet the assumption that we can gain security by reducing liberty is profoundly misleading. One reason is the point so often stressed by civil libertarians—that security, properly understood, encompasses our freedom. A surveillance society that places public safety over all other concerns inevitably chills political freedom, constrains creativity, and inhibits our personal lives. Pervasive surveillance, no less than the dangers of terrorism, corrodes the fabric of a vibrant, healthy civic life.

But the "balancing" metaphor is also deceptive in ways that should concern even the most safety-minded citizen. Many people support surveillance, despite its chilling effects, because their highest priority is to prevent a catastrophic attack. Like Judge Posner, they typically fail to see that reducing our liberty can *diminish* our safety.

Focusing on a "liberty-security trade-off" can actually impair security because it tends to obscure *better* ways to prevent attacks— for example, hiring more agents who understand foreign languages, or placing cement barriers in front of buildings that are likely targets. Of course, options like these do not in themselves make the balancing metaphor inaccurate, because we can take many steps simultaneously. We can recruit more translators, harden vulnerable targets, *and* enhance government surveillance powers. But our political system is seldom able to do more than a few things at the same time. Invariably, we prioritize. And when we spotlight one set of solutions, others inevitably command less attention and fewer resources.

Measures that might make us a bit safer (for example, by reducing safeguards for privacy) therefore become positively harmful if they divert attention from issues that matter much more. And constant emphasis on a supposed liberty-security trade-off distorts our priorities in just that way. It leads us to think first of restricting civil liberties and to think less (or not at all) about steps that can be far more effective.

That tendency is especially strong because the "restrict liberty" solution is usually simple to implement. Protecting vulnerable ports and chemical plants is difficult and expensive. Training more CIA agents to speak Urdu or Pashtun takes time, and finding native speakers who can qualify for security clearance is even thornier. Compared to other remedies, conferring more surveillance power is easy, and it seems cheap. With pencil, paper, and a roll-call vote, the solution is achieved almost overnight. And it meets the first obligation of elected officials in a time of crisis—the obligation to *do something*.

The difficulty is that the rollback of civil liberties, though seemingly vigorous and tough, can easily dissipate the political will to address more important issues. Fortunately, the Patriot Act did not divert attention from the urgency of better airport security and other especially obvious target-hardening requirements. But the Act nonetheless pushed many significant problems to the back burner or off the agenda entirely.

Consider the 9/11 Commission's diagnosis of the intelligence failures leading up to the 9/11 attacks. In page after page of analysis and recommendations, the Commission mentioned problems in organization, training, and execution throughout the government. But nowhere did the Commission cite an absence of surveillance authority as a relevant weakness in the events leading up to 9/11. As is evident throughout the report, and painful to read, the government possessed an enormous amount of alarming information prior to 9/11. Unfortunately, as many intelligence agents later acknowledged, "we didn't know what we knew." The only legal problem that the 9/11 Commission mentioned at all was what those in the intelligence field had called the "wall," the separation between prosecutors and intelligence agents that became a frequent scapegoat in media accounts of pre-9/11 failures. Yet the Commission concluded that the "wall" was primarily a product of bureaucratic culture, turf protection, inadequate training, and poor understanding of legal rules—not a product of the legal rules themselves. Several followup assessments in the years since 9/11 make clear that despite much progress, many of our most consequential weaknesses remain uncorrected.*

Civil liberties myopia makes us vulnerable in other ways as well. In a successful intelligence effort, information must be gathered, translated, shared with the relevant agencies, analyzed insightfully, and then delivered promptly to officials in a position to act. Stronger surveillance powers do help with the first step. But if we lack sufficient agents to translate and analyze the intelligence collected, the additional "take" is useless—or worse. True, a small nugget of information can sometimes provide the key to decoding an entire picture. But as agents pull in more and more of these nuggets, it becomes harder for analysts, especially understaffed analysts, to spot that telling detail among the ever increasing clutter of background noise. Piling more hay on a haystack is not the best way to help an analyst find the needle. The assumption that a little more information might just help, and can never hurt, is perilously oversimplified.

Our traditional Fourth Amendment oversight framework evolved in part as a response to this very problem. By setting a threshold of relevance and requiring review by a disinterested court, the Fourth

---

* For an especially disturbing recent assessment, see U.S. Senate, Committee on Homeland Security and Governmental Affairs, *"A Ticking Time Bomb": Counterterrorism Lessons from the U.S. Government's Failure to Prevent the Fort Hood Attack* (February 3, 2011).

Amendment prevents wasteful mission creep and restrains investigators' tendency to cast ever wider information-gathering nets. By limiting the predictable but counterproductive executive appetite for unbounded amounts of intelligence, the amendment has served for centuries as a mechanism to enhance *both* liberty and security. As the Supreme Court noted in insisting on respect for the warrant requirement even in national security investigations:

> The warrant clause...is not an inconvenience to be somehow "weighed" against the claims of police efficiency. It is, or should be, an important working part of our machinery of government, operating as a matter of course to check the well-intentioned but mistakenly overzealous executive officers who are a part of any system of law enforcement.... [U]nreviewed executive discretion may yield too readily to pressures to obtain incriminating evidence....[21]

It is therefore a fundamental error to suppose that the Bill of Rights only protects individuals and minority groups, rather than the wider community. Civil liberties serve broader purposes. One, of course, is the benefit that everyone derives from living in a free society that shelters personal privacy, religious freedom, and political dissent. Less obviously, civil liberties enhance our physical safety and protect us from attack.

In times of danger, it is human nature to react quickly and instinctively. Public officials are not immune to that tendency, and sometimes it can serve us well. But when their responses to a threat are excessive or poorly targeted, their efforts can backfire.

The military analogy, though often overused, can be helpful here. An army unit under fire does not want an officer so inhibited that he is unwilling to order a counterattack. But it also does not want one who reacts instinctively and commits his forces prematurely or in the wrong place; precipitous action often is exactly what the enemy hopes to entice, and it is usually the prelude to military disaster. An effective fighter must be willing to fire but also must know how to aim. Military command is therefore first and foremost an exercise in assessing the big picture and weighing alternatives, not simply unleashing brute force.

Hospitals offer a similar lesson. In a crisis, doctors and nurses do not throw away the rule book. They stick to preestablished protocols, because experience has shown that precipitous action, the impulse to simply *do something*, leads to life-endangering errors. As political scientist Stephen Holmes observes:

> Emergency-room personnel are acutely aware of the serious risks posed by excessive delay. Though they understand the need for immediate and unhesitating action, they nevertheless routinely consume precious time to follow protocols drilled into them and practiced in advance.... They do it to minimize the risk of making fatal-but-avoidable mistakes under the psychologically flustering pressures of the moment.[22]

In responding to the challenge of terrorism, we have too often disregarded these lessons. Fear has led much of the American public to assume that checks on the executive branch endanger our security. But oversight and accountability—two essential pillars of our constitutional tradition—do not make us more vulnerable to attack. In counterterrorism, as in every other area of law enforcement and public protection, the goal of Fourth Amendment safeguards is not to block government intrusions altogether but only to keep them well-targeted. In this respect, our civil liberties do not conflict with our safety, and we cannot "balance" one against the other. Oversight—however much government investigators may resist it—makes a crucial contribution to the success of the national security mission.

MISTRUST AND ALIENATION

Perhaps even more important, successful law enforcement requires wholehearted community support. When people see suspicious activity or discover a criminal in hiding, they have to decide whether to alert the police. They may also be asked to attend meetings to discuss policing strategy or to participate in a neighborhood watch. Yet it is easy for people to choose not to cooperate. They will not help unless they *want to*. And criminal justice research consistently finds that willingness to assist the police is strong only when people believe that officials can be trusted to exercise their authority fairly.[23]

The same is true, only more so, with efforts to combat terrorism. Because terrorism threatens so many possible targets and because its operatives typically have no prior record of terrorist activity, accurate and timely information is especially important for separating genuine threats from background noise. That information can conceivably come from a surveillance intercept, but crucial warnings often come from law-abiding citizens in the community. Such cooperation is fragile, because these citizens, though unswervingly opposed to violence, know that their tip might bring harsh procedures and sanctions to bear on people with whom they share close ethnic and religious ties.

In the weeks and months after 9/11, with public discourse driven by widespread anxiety, and with heightened awareness of the genuine threats that the United States now faced, many commentators urged wider use of police checkpoints, searches, and ethnic profiling. They supported more surveillance of phone calls, email and private records, with greater flexibility for investigators and reduced oversight. In more recent years, expert assessments of the terrorist threat have changed, but public fears have scarcely abated. And perhaps understandably so. No doubt, "al Qaeda Central" has been greatly weakened, and of course Osama Bin Laden has been killed. But al Qaeda spin-offs and smaller cells seem to have proliferated around the world. And "homegrown" Islamic terrorism, once considered a remote prospect United States, has now surfaced as a significant, widespread domestic phenomenon.[24]

These developments have sustained and even reinforced public support for intensive law enforcement, pervasive surveillance, and reduced oversight of anti-terror efforts. Yet such steps can be exceptionally shortsighted because they sow the seeds of mistrust in many parts of our population. In Ann Arbor, Michigan, a city with a substantial Muslim-American population, the Muslim Community Association was forced to file suit against the Department of Justice because, like many such organizations, it was facing intrusive FBI demands for access to its membership records.[25] In Tennessee, an agency of the World Church Service, one of the leading Protestant umbrella organizations for refugee relief, discovered that the threat of FBI access to its records was discouraging donors and preventing many immigrants from seeking its assistance.[26] Yet as we have seen in chapter 6, the "third-party doctrine," as currently interpreted, gives no Fourth Amendment protection for such material.

No doubt investigative measures like these can sometimes generate valuable information. But for every useful bit of intelligence they produce, they can choke off dozens or hundreds of others, because they fuel resentment and chill cooperation in the targeted communities—communities whose loyalty and support have become all the more important as "homegrown" threats have grown in significance.

Paying this price is especially imprudent because it is almost always unnecessary. We need not choose between getting information through surveillance and getting it through citizen cooperation. Usually we can pursue both, preserving community trust and the cooperation it generates, simply by keeping the normal Fourth Amendment system in place—not prohibiting surveillance but merely insisting that it meet reasonable standards under independent oversight. Proposals to forego that protection—to relax Fourth Amendment requirements and "trade off" liberty for security—make counterterrorism efforts more difficult, not less.

Post 9/11 research provides stark warnings about this danger. Extensive studies of Muslim American residents of New York City find (contrary to much conventional wisdom) that religiosity, cultural differences, and political background have little impact on willingness to assist in antiterrorism efforts. But cooperation is strongly affected by whether authorities are perceived as trustworthy and fair. Even when Muslim Americans consider the terror threat very serious, willingness to cooperate drops substantially if they believe the police are targeting people in their community, stopping people without explanation, denying them any opportunity to be heard, and failing to treat them with courtesy. Regardless of prior attitudes about the police or civil liberties, these perceptions of fairness have a major effect on willingness to cooperate.[27]

The heart of the national security challenge—the reason it seems to make ordinary Fourth Amendment safeguards too costly—is the extraordinary nature of the threat and the concern that "we simply cannot afford to take chances." But the liberty-security dynamic (it is not a "balance") makes clear that *there are no risk-free choices.* Strengthening the powers of the executive enhances some of our defenses against terrorism, but it *weakens* many of our most important means of protection.

Worldwide, there are at most only a few thousand Islamic extremists determined to do us harm. But there are more than a million law-abiding Muslims in the United States and more than a billion worldwide. To combat terrorism successfully, the support of these communities is imperative. Unless our laws foster trust by guaranteeing transparency and accountability, strong search and surveillance authority quickly becomes self-defeating. If we succumb to seductive calls for unchecked intelligence-gathering powers, while devoting insufficient attention to the resource deficits and organizational weaknesses that plague our national security effort, we cannot be safe, no matter how much of our liberty we are willing to sacrifice.

. . .

CHAPTER EIGHT

The Fourth Amendment Today: Misunderstood but Indispensable

UNDER SIEGE FOR SEVERAL DECADES in the Supreme Court, in legislative bodies and in the public mind, Fourth Amendment safeguards no longer ensure the opportunities for personal security that the Framers considered essential for individual freedom and political democracy. The attacks of September 11, 2011, gave law enforcement officials new reasons to seek relief from Fourth Amendment strictures; fear of terrorism has prompted public opinion to tolerate and even encourage their demands. But these recent developments merely reinforce trends that have persisted for decades, fueled by the "war on drugs" and, before that, the "war on crime" and the law-and-order politics of the 1960s and 1970s.

Still, polling consistently shows that Americans remain deeply wary of unrestrained government power. Most of us dread pervasive surveillance; we are unwilling to allow officials unchecked authority to seize individuals or rummage through personal effects. In short, we cherish privacy and personal autonomy. Their value is obvious, incontestable. Yet their importance is simultaneously obscure, disputed, dismissed. For the public at large, instincts conflict; responses are erratic. And the justices of the Supreme Court do no better. At bottom, when it comes to the what, how, and why— what the Fourth Amendment protects, how and why it gives that protection—understandings are poor.

The tendency to favor investigative powers and disapprove of legal restraints often begins with the assumption that the point of the Fourth Amendment is to shield misconduct. After all, the Framers themselves were rebels; they evaded taxation and plotted to overthrow their colonial governments. Today, marijuana users, hard-core drug kingpins, distributors of child pornography, and the like are often in the lead of those who most visibly seek Fourth Amendment protection. Terrorists hoping to commit mass murder claim its benefits. President George W. Bush, objecting to legal constraints on electronic surveillance, often said, in effect, "When al Qaeda calls, we want to listen."[1] Small wonder that Fourth Amendment requirements often garner little public support. They seem like a gift to those bent on wrongdoing, offering nothing but inconvenience or danger to the law-abiding public. Why worry about searches and surveillance if you have nothing to hide?

This is a profound misconception. Far from shielding the guilty, the Fourth Amendment aims to do precisely the opposite. It is carefully structured to *exclude* the guilty from its shelter. As we have seen throughout this book, the Fourth Amendment *permits* searches and seizures—it declares that privacy is lost—when a magistrate finds probable cause to suspect illegality.

Unlike freedom of religion or the privilege against self-incrimination, therefore, privacy is not unconditionally shielded from deliberate government interference. The Fourth Amendment only protects the privacy of citizens *not* reasonably suspected of misconduct. When al Qaeda calls, surveillance is perfectly permissible.

In aiming to protect tranquility and personal security, the Fourth Amendment proceeds by *regulating*, by insisting on independent *oversight*. Through its requirements of probable cause and a warrant, it seeks to ensure that officials empowered to search for crime do not use their authority so carelessly or aggressively that law-abiding citizens are unnecessarily made to feel vulnerable.

To be sure, our Fourth Amendment tradition attributes special importance to privacy. But its core preoccupation is with the threat posed by unchecked executive power. It recognizes privacy as an essential component of individual happiness, but it also reflects a judgment about the conditions for sound government—that judicial oversight is the best way to assure that alleged law enforcement requirements are indeed legitimate and that vital but dangerous investigative powers do not *unjustifiably* intrude on fundamental freedoms. The *what* of Fourth Amendment protection, in short, is both personal and institutional: privacy—a fundamental human right—is guaranteed, but not absolutely; the amendment's primary concern is to safeguard privacy from *abuses of executive discretion*.

The contemporary Supreme Court often honors that commitment, especially when intrusions affect the interior of the home. But outside the home, the Court far too often makes police convenience its priority. Deference to law enforcement discretion has dominated the Court's decisions in countless areas: warrantless arrests, warrantless searches of cars, stops and searches based on a fictitious "consent," pretext arrests for minor traffic infractions, searches of private records entrusted to institutions, "administrative" checkpoints, and mandatory urinalysis testing, to name a few.

By insisting time and again on deference to the police and other executive authorities, the Court has in effect stood our Fourth Amendment tradition on its head, treating oversight of law enforcement discretion as illegitimate judicial activism. But such oversight is precisely what the Framers intended. Unchecked discretion and judicial deference to law enforcement is exactly what the Framers sought to preclude. The famous English decisions that gave birth to our Fourth Amendment put the point plainly: "It is not fit, that the...judging of the information should be left to the discretion of the officer. The magistrate ought to judge."[2]

The contemporary Court's departure from this original understanding is clear enough, but fair-minded enforcement of the Fourth Amendment remains a challenge for any Supreme Court justice, because so many dimensions of privacy and law enforcement differ today from anything the Framers imagined. Does respect for their intentions require the Court to apply the search-and-seizure rules that the Framers knew in the eighteenth century? Or does it require the Court to adapt those rules, so that the Framers' underlying objectives can be realized in changing circumstances? In other words, does "originalism" require the Court to respect original *rules* or original *principles*? Does originalism allow for—or require—adaptation?

ORIGINALISM AND ADAPTATION

Self-described originalists like Justice Antonin Scalia typically insist that the Court must apply only the constitutional rules that the Framers themselves contemplated, because they believe that turning to broader principles will leave the Court free to pick its own preferred outcomes. The Fourth Amendment has posed this problem in dozens of settings. And the Court's practice makes clear that the issue has only one possible answer. Although the Court occasionally insists that it must apply search-and-seizure rules as originally formulated, and acts as if this were the only legitimate choice, we have seen in these pages that all of the justices (including Scalia) opt repeatedly for adaptation.

The catch is that adaptation has almost always been a one-way street. The Court frequently abandons eighteenth-century search-and-seizure requirements and prefers adaptation when it finds the old rules at odds with new law enforcement needs. It rarely opts for adaptation when that approach would restrict police discretion.

Exceptions to this pattern should be acknowledged. The Court holds that police cannot use deadly force to apprehend a fleeing felon who has not endangered life, even though that use of deadly force was permissible in the eighteenth century. Without a warrant, police cannot eavesdrop on conversations or analyze heat patterns emanating from a house (actions they were free to attempt in the eighteenth century) if they use modern electronic devices to assist them.

More often, however, when modern circumstances jeopardize personal security and informational privacy in new ways, the Court declines to limit police discretion. Sophisticated technologies pose the most obvious of these problems. The Court refuses to afford Fourth Amendment safeguards against the use of helicopters and other aircraft to observe activities in the backyard of the home, and it denies protection against the use of electronic beepers to track short-term movements on public streets.

The more important difficulties, however, arise from social, not technological change. It is there that new developments have been most dramatic and most threatening to privacy. Law enforcement in the eighteenth century was almost exclusively the province of unarmed or poorly armed part-time amateurs, and only the most serious, life-threatening offenses were considered felonies for which a constable could make a warrantless arrest. Citizens seldom traveled any distance, there were few traffic laws enforceable by arrest, and no highway patrol was ready to pounce in the event of a violation. In those conditions, the Framers could rightly assume that broad common-law powers to arrest conferred little discretion and few opportunities for abuse. Our world bears almost no similarity to that one. The "felony" label now attaches to dozens of crimes, many of them minor property offenses that carry light sentences. Well-armed police officers are a constant presence on our sidewalks, streets and interstate highways. Most Americans spend significant portions of their day in their cars, where the vehicle code subjects them to arrest at almost any time for a host of minor infractions. The eighteenth-century assumption that common-law arrest powers constrain discretion and prevent abusive interference with freedom of movement is laughably out of date.

Yet the Court has scarcely budged. Acting as if the old common-law rules are carved in stone, beyond the Court's legitimate powers to modify, the Court permits warrantless arrests for any offense that carries the "felony" label. It allows police to make pretext arrests for any traffic infraction, no matter how trivial, even when their motivation admittedly is not to enforce the traffic laws but only to pursue suspicions of drug trafficking for which they have no objective justification. It upholds searches on the basis of "voluntary" consent, even when armed officers with broad coercive powers give the citizen no hint that she is free to refuse. Common-law rules that once conferred little discretion now give the police sweeping authority to intrude on the ordinary citizen's freedom and security in public places.

The real justification for these decisions may simply be the Court's perception that police officers can be trusted to exercise discretion fairly without close oversight. If so, that assumption runs directly counter to the Fourth Amendment's central commitments—to sheltering private spaces from government intrusion, assuring judicial checks, and preventing unlimited executive discretion, whether it be exercised by untrained low-level agents or by officials like Lord Halifax, who held the highest rank and social status.

A similar, one-sided rigidity, exalting formal rules and ignoring their practical effect when they favor law enforcement, has dominated in the Court's approach to shared information. The Court has insisted that personal details revealed confidentially to a third party are no longer "private" and that the Fourth Amendment therefore gives the government unregulated access to them. This principle had little impact on privacy in early America, where citizens typically shared information only within a small circle of trusted associates. Even in the 1970s, communication still consisted primarily of hard-copy letters and conversations conducted in person or by telephone. Today, social and professional life is impossible without transmitting personal correspondence, financial records, and personal documents through ISPs, banks, and data processing centers. Yet the "third-party doctrine" that the Court often invokes seems to leave us powerless to shield ourselves from unregulated government scrutiny of this information, even when we choose intermediaries that offer commitments of confidentiality that they strive to honor. To keep the government at arm's length, our only alternative is to withdraw entirely from community life.

We can only speculate about whether the Framers would have accepted the "third-party doctrine" in their own day, but we can be certain they would not have tolerated its implications for life in the twenty-first century. They sought to create a charter of government that protects personal development and civic engagement, not one that requires us to become hermits.

All this, a rule-based originalist might say, is unfortunate but beyond the Court's control, because the Court (she might say) has no license to keep the Constitution "in tune with the times." Yet this is precisely what the Court does when government officials assert a need for more discretion than the old common-law rules allowed. Does the density of modern cities pose fire and health hazards that the Framers never anticipated? Then a warrant authorizing search of an entire area, something the Framers undoubtedly abhorred, is now permissible. Does drunk driving or an influx of immigrants present a new social problem? Then the Fourth Amendment permits a checkpoint to stop all travelers, regardless of individual suspicion or probable cause. Does drug use by airline pilots or high school athletes or even high school flute players produce dangers the Framers did not foresee? Then citizens not suspected of any offense can now be compelled to submit to intrusive urinalysis drug testing.

To limit modern governments to the particulars of eighteenth-century search-and-seizure rules is not always necessary to keep faith with the underlying values that the Framers cherished. And the Court has rightly recognized as much. "Administrative" searches are properly upheld when they respond to pressing new problems in a way that honors underlying Fourth Amendment principles—by preserving judicial oversight, constraining discretion, and sacrificing individual privacy only to the extent necessary.

This is *adaptive* originalism, appropriate and unavoidable. But it cannot with any logic or intellectual honesty be defined as a one-way street. To assume that officials can be trusted to exercise intrusive powers without oversight—to permit law enforcement discretion steadily to expand, while leaving individual citizens with only the protective shields that sufficed in the eighteenth century (the walls of the home and the opaque envelopes of sealed correspondence)—is to make a policy judgment diametrically opposed to the one on which the Fourth Amendment rests. This is what the Court rightly recognized in the wiretap setting, but in recent decades the Court has seemed to lose sight of this foundational principle.

MORE ESSENTIAL THAN EVER: OVERSIGHT,
AND LAW ENFORCEMENT RESTRAINT

And yet, and yet...

For many Americans, the skepticism remains. Especially when dangers lurk, why are vigorous government efforts to detect and preempt them objectionable? Why is the opportunity to preserve secrecy so important if you are not violating the law?

Part of the answer lies in the essential preconditions for individual growth and fulfillment. Imagine a world in which none of us—however respectable—could ever claim a refuge where we felt free from observation. Suspicion of unrestrained government power runs deep in American culture, and understandably so. Whatever people may express in moments when they feel frightened and in need of protection, the message of conflicts between government and the individual throughout history is clear: The ability to control what we reveal about ourselves and to whom is essential for having a sense of personal peace, for trying out new ideas, and for developing our potential. Justice Robert Jackson, fresh from serving as chief U.S. prosecutor at the Nuremberg war crimes trials, saw the experience of Nazi Germany and invoked it in his Fourth Amendment opinions on his return to the Court: "Among deprivations of rights, none is so effective in cowing a population, crushing the spirit of the individual and putting terror in every heart. [D]ignity and self-reliance disappear where homes, persons and possessions are subject at any hour to unheralded search and seizure."[3] Even for the most conventional among us, *personal autonomy*—the ability to flourish as an independent individual—cannot survive in the absence of opportunities for privacy.

There are wider effects as well. Most of us who lead ordinary lives and have "nothing to hide" nonetheless hope to live in a society where creative individuals can innovate and produce the unexpected—in business, in literature, in entertainment. Even if we feel no intense need for privacy ourselves, other people do, and we all reap the benefits of a culture that nurtures their individuality. As Justice Jackson recognized, pervasive surveillance stifles creativity and erodes the vitality of community life.

The political implications are equally fundamental. Democracy requires skeptics, those who question conventional wisdom, criticize, or dissent. Yet when the government knows everything that people read or do and whom they associate with, the ability to join with like-minded skeptics weakens dramatically. The ability to express disagreement effectively and to support unpopular causes atrophies. Those who find prevailing views congenial, or who simply take no interest in politics, may not consider government surveillance personally intimidating. But at all points on the political spectrum, and even among those who are not politically engaged, Americans recognize the importance of freedom of speech and association. And those freedoms cannot thrive, cannot even survive, in the absence of private spaces and protected relationships in which they can be pursued. So the Fourth Amendment holds an indispensable place in the American constitutional design. It guarantees the essential buffer between outsiders of all sorts and the power of the state. Unrestricted search and surveillance powers undermine politics and impoverish personal, social, and cultural life in ways that affect all of us. Everyone needs the Fourth Amendment.

As we have seen throughout this book, these concerns do not require us to keep personal records and activities absolutely beyond the government's reach. Fourth Amendment principles only require guarantees of *restraint*—to ensure that government's powerful investigative tools will be used properly, with meaningful oversight. In this regard, the changing circumstances of our world in the twenty-first century have not made Fourth Amendment safeguards less important. On the contrary.

Technology and our evolving relationship with it have increased our dependence on intermediaries to whom we inevitably must entrust our private records and communications. Opportunities for self-sufficiency that were available as recently as ten or twenty years ago are rapidly evaporating. International instability and the proliferation of small, easily carried weapons with enormous destructive potential have exposed our communities to new threats and led us, often with justification, to grant new investigatory powers to the government.

Yet human nature has not changed, and the ability to find refuge from the all-seeing eye of Big Brother remains as important as ever. As our private spaces become more transparent and as the government's surveillance powers increase, independent judicial oversight—in short, the Fourth Amendment—becomes more essential than ever.

The Framers of our Constitution sought to afford every citizen the opportunity to claim a sheltered area, free of indiscriminate government spying, as an indispensable foundation for personal and political freedom. Today more than ever, we must insist that our leaders, and above all the justices of our Supreme Court, fulfill their constitutional obligations by preserving Fourth Amendment values and adapting its safeguards so as to enable all of us to protect our privacy in the rapidly changing conditions of modern life.

Notes

...

CHAPTER ONE

1. Richard A. Posner, *Not a Suicide Pact* (New York: Oxford University Press, 2006), p. 141.
2. William J. Stuntz, "Secret Service: Against Privacy and Transparency," *The New Republic*, April 17, 2006, p. 12.
3. Soldal v. Cook County, 506 U.S. 56 (1992).
4. Katz v. United States, 389 U.S. 347 (1967).
5. Stoner v. California, 376 U.S. 483 (1964).
6. Smith v. Maryland, 442 U.S. 735, 743–44 (1979).
7. United States v. Miller, 425 U.S. 435 (1976).
8. Incal v. Turkey, 29 Eur. H.R. Rep. 449, 480 (1998).
9. *Katz*, supra.

CHAPTER TWO

1. Quoted in Nelson B. Lasson, *The History and Development of the Fourth Amendment to the United States Constitution* (Baltimore, Md.: The Johns Hopkins Press, 1937), p. 15.

2. Sir Matthew Hale, *History of the Pleas of the Crown*, ed. Sollom Emlyn, vol. 2 (London: E. Rider, Little-Britain, 1800), p. 150. Hale's commentary was written prior to 1676 (the year of his death) but first published in 1736. See Thomas Y. Davies, "Recovering the Original Fourth Amendment," *Michigan Law Review* 98 (1999): 579 note 75.

3. Quoted in Lasson, p. 42.

4. The terms of the warrant are quoted in full in Arthur Cash, *John Wilkes: The Scandalous Father of Civil Liberty* (New Haven, Conn.: Yale University Press, 2006), p. 101.

5. Quoted in Lasson, p. 44 note 109.

6. Huckle v. Money, 95 Eng. Rep. 768, 769 (Common Pleas 1763).

7. Id. See Lasson, pp. 44–45 and note 111.

8. Wilkes v. Wood, 19 Howell's State Trials 1153, 1167 (Common Pleas 1763), fully quoted in Lasson, p. 45.

9. Boyd v. United States, 116 U.S. 616, 625–30 (1886).

10. Entick v. Carrington, 95 Eng. Rep. 807, 817–18; 19 Howell's State Trials 1029, 1066 (Common Pleas 1765).

11. Quoted in M. H. Smith, *The Writs of Assistance Case* (Berkeley.: University of California Press, 1978), p. 553 (italics in original omitted).

12. Quoted in id., p. 553. The complete text of Otis's argument, as transcribed by John Adams, is reprinted in id., pp. 551–55.

13. Id., pp. 552, 554.

14. Quoted in Lasson, p. 59.

15. See Akhil Reed Amar, "Fourth Amendment First Principles," *Harvard Law Review* 107 (1994): 757.

16. See Davies, pp. 619–68.

17. Quoted in Smith, p. 553.

18. Quoted in Davies, p. 589 note 104.

19. Entick v. Carrington, 95 Eng. Rep. at 812.

20. Quoted in *Legal Papers of John Adams*, ed. L. Kinvin Wroth & Hiller B. Zobel, vol. 2 (Cambridge, Mass.: Harvard University Press 1965), p. 142.

21. Hale, vol. 2, p. 150.

22. William Hawkins, *Pleas of the Crown*, Book II, 2d ed. (London: E. & R. Nutt and R. Gosling, 1726), p. 82.

23. Wilkes v. Wood, p. 1167.

24. Leach v. Three of the King's Messengers, 19 Howell's State Trials 1001, 1027 (King's Bench 1765).

25. Blackstone said that "a *general* warrant…is illegal and void for its uncertainty…; for it…ought not be left to the officer, to judge of the grounds of suspicion." William Blackstone, *Commentaries on the Laws of England*, vol. 4 (1769, facsimile ed., Chicago: University of Chicago Press, 1979), p. 288.
26. See Davies, pp. 581–82.
27. See id., pp. 686–93.

CHAPTER THREE

The epigraph to this chapter is from Brinegar v. United States, 338 U.S. 160, 180–81 (1949) (Jackson, J., dissenting).
1. United States v. United States District Court, 407 U.S. 297, 317 (1972).
2. Richards v. Wisconsin, 520 U.S. 385 (1997).
3. Hudson v. Michigan, 547 U.S. 586 (2006).
4. Compare Dalia v. United States, 441 U.S. 238 (1979), where the Court held that covert entry and delayed notice are permissible when necessary for the installation of secret surveillance devices.
5. Warden v. Hayden, 387 U.S. 294 (1967).
6. Vale v. Louisiana, 399 U.S. 30 (1970).
7. Minnesota v. Olson, 495 U.S. 91 (1990).
8. United States v. Watson, 423 U.S. 411, 418 (1976).
9. Tennessee v. Garner, 471 U.S. 1, 11, 13 (1985).
10. Coker v. Georgia, 433 U.S. 584 (1977); Kennedy v. Louisiana, 554 U.S. 407 (2008).
11. Woodson v. North Carolina, 428 U.S. 280 (1976); Sumner v. Shuman, 483 U.S. 66 (1987).
12. United States v. Chadwick, 433 U.S. 1 (1977).
13. Chambers v. Maroney, 399 U.S. 42 (1970).
14. California v. Carney, 471 U.S. 386 (1985).
15. Chimel v. California, 395 U.S. 752 (1969).
16. New York v. Belton, 453 U.S. 454 (1981).
17. Arizona v. Gant, 556 U.S. 332 (2009).
18. Schneckloth v. Bustamonte, 412 U.S. 218 (1973).
19. Whren v. United States, 517 U.S. 806 (1996).

20. Atwater v. City of Lago Vista, 532 U.S. 318 (2001).
21. Weeks v. United States, 232 U.S. 383 (1914).
22. Mapp v. Ohio, 367 U.S. 643 (1961).
23. United States v. Calandra, 414 U.S. 338, 357 (1974) Brennan, J., dissenting).
24. Olmstead v. United States, 277 U.S. 438, 485 (1928) (Brandeis, J., dissenting).
25. United States v. Leon, 468 U.S. 897, 907 (1984).
26. Hudson v. Michigan, 547 U.S. 586, 591, 596 (2006).
27. Herring v. United States, 555 U.S. 135, 144 (2009).
28. Wolf v. Colorado, 338 U.S. 25, 41 (1949) (dissenting opinion).
29. See David Alan Sklansky, "Is the Exclusionary Rule Obsolete?" *Ohio State Journal of Criminal Law* 5 (2008): 579–82.
30. Stephen J. Schulhofer, Tom R. Tyler, and Aziz Huq, "American Policing at a Crossroads: Unsustainable Policies and the Procedural Justice Alternative," *Journal of Criminal Law and Criminology* 101 (2011): 335.

CHAPTER FOUR

The epigraph to this chapter is a quotation from Papachristou v. City of Jacksonville, 405 U.S. 156, 164, 170–71 (1972).
1. Mapp v. Ohio, 367 U.S. 643 (1961).
2. Terry v. Ohio, 392 U.S. 1 (1968).
3. Id. at 16–17 and note 13.
4. Id. at 14–15.
5. *Papachristou*, supra.
6. Coates v. City of Cincinnati, 402 U.S. 611 (1971).
7. Shuttlesworth v. City of Birmingham, 382 U.S. 87 (1965).
8. City of Chicago v. Morales, 527 U.S. 41 (1999).
9. Id. at 109 (Thomas, J., dissenting).
10. Stephen J. Schulhofer, Tom R. Tyler, and Aziz Huq, "American Policing at a Crossroads: Unsustainable Policies and the Procedural Justice Alternative," *Journal of Criminal Law and Criminology* 101 (2011): 335.
11. *Terry*, supra at 13.
12. Id. at 16.

13. United States v. Mendenhall, 446 U.S. 544, 554 (1980) (opinion of Stewart, J.).
14. INS v. Delgado, 466 U.S. 210, 218 (1984).
15. Id. at 231 (dissenting opinion).
16. Id. at 229.
17. Florida v. Bostick, 501 U.S. 429 (1991); United States v. Drayton, 536 U.S. 194 (2002).
18. California v. Hodari D., 499 U.S. 621 (1991).
19. Katz v. United States, 389 U.S. 347 (1967).
20. United States v. Jones, 2012 U.S. LEXIS 1063, at *20 (U.S., Jan. 23, 2012) ("We do not make trespass the exclusive test. Situations involving merely the transmission of electronic signals without trespass...*remain* subject to *Katz* analysis); Kyllo v. United States, 533 U.S. 27 (2001).
21. Illinois v. Wardlow, 528 U.S. 119 (2000).
22. Andrew Gelman et al., "An Analysis of the New York City Police Department's 'Stop and Frisk' Policy in the Context of Claims of Racial Bias," *Journal of the American Statistical Association* 102 (2007): 813, 816, 820. See also Jeffrey Fagan et al., "Street Stops and Broken Windows Revisited," in S. K. Rice and M. D. White, eds., *Race, Ethnicity and Policing* (New York: New York University Press, 2010), 309, 321, 332.

CHAPTER FIVE

The epigraph to this chapter is from Olmstead v. United States, 277 U.S. 438, 479 (1928) (Brandeis, J., dissenting).
1. Camara v. Municipal Court, 387 U.S. 523 (1967).
2. Id at 537.
3. District of Columbia v. Little, 178 F.2d 13, 16–17 (D.C. Cir. 1949).
4. See Stephen J. Schulhofer, "On the Fourth Amendment Rights of the Law-Abiding Public," *Supreme Court Review* 87 (1989): 87–163.
5. National Treasury Employees Union v. Von Raab, 489 U.S. 656, 665 (1989).
6. Marshall v. Barlow's, Inc., 436 U.S. 307 (1978); Donovan v. Dewey, 452 U.S. 594 (1981).
7. Chandler v. Miller, 520 U.S. 305, 323 (1997).
8. Id. at 318, 322 (emphasis added).

9. New York v. Burger, 482 U.S. 691 (1987).

10. Id. at 713–14, 717.

11. Griffin v. Wisconsin, 483 U.S. 868 (1987).

12. Id. at 873–74.

13. Id. at 876.

14. Veronia School District 47J v. Acton, 515 U.S. 646, 671 (1995) (O'Connor, J., dissenting).

15. City of Indianapolis v. Edmond, 531 U.S. 32 (2000).

16. United States v. Martinez-Fuerte, 428 U.S. 543 (1976).

17. Michigan Dep't of State Police v. Sitz, 496 U.S. 444 (1990).

18. Edmond, 531 US at 56 (dissenting opinion).

19. Skinner v. Railway Labor Executives' Ass'n, 489 U.S. 602 (1989).

20. Ferguson v. City of Charleston, 532 U.S. 67 (2001).

21. Chandler v. Miller, 520 U.S. 305 (1997).

22. New Jersey v. T.L.O., 469 U.S. 325, 342 (1985).

23. Safford Unified School District No. 1 v. Redding, 129 S. Ct. 2633, 2643 (2009).

24. Veronia, supra.

25. Id. at 686 (O'Connor, J. dissenting).

26. Board of Education v. Earls, 536 U.S. 822, 832 (2002).

27. Id. at 834.

28. Id. at 845 (Ginsburg, J., dissenting).

29. Id. at 852.

30. Id.

31. New Jersey v. T.L.O., 469 U.S. 325, 340 (1985).

CHAPTER SIX

The epigraph for this chapter is from Olmstead v. United States, 277 U.S. 438, 474 (1928) (Brandeis, J., dissenting).

1. Olmstead v. United States, 277 U.S. 438, 464 (1928).

2. Id. at 473, 476, 478 (Brandeis, J., dissenting).

3. Entick v. Carrington, 95 Eng. Rep. 807, 818; 19 Howell's State Trials 1029, 1066 (Common Pleas 1765).

4. Goldman v. United States, 316 U.S. 129 (1942).

5. Silverman v. United States, 365 U.S. 505 (1961).

6. Id. at 513 (Douglas, J., concurring).

7. Katz v. United States, 389 U.S. 347, 351 (1967).

8. Id. at 352.

9. Id. at 360 (Harlan, J., concurring).

10. Kyllo v. United States, 533 U.S. 27, 37 (2001) (emphasis in original).

11. United States v. Karo, 468 U.S. 705 (1984).

12. United States v. Knotts, 460 U.S. 276 (1983).

13. United States v. Miller, 425 U.S. 435 (1976).

14. Smith v. Maryland, 442 U.S. 735, 744 (1979).

15. California v. Ciraolo, 476 U.S. 207 (1986).

16. Florida v. Riley, 488 U.S. 445 (1989).

17. *Katz*, supra at 352.

18. *Smith v. Maryland*, supra, 442 U.S. at 744.

19. *Miller*, supra.

20. United States v. Warshak, 631 F.3d 266 (6th Cir. 2010).

21. Richard A. Posner, *Not a Suicide Pact* (New York: Oxford University Press, 2006), p. 140.

22. O'Connor v. Ortega, 480 U.S. 709, 730 (1987) (Scalia, J., concurring).

23. See Claire Cain Miller, "Another Try by Google to Take On Facebook," *New York Times*, June 28, 2011; Nick Bilton, "Privacy Isn't Dead. Just Ask Google+," *New York Times online*, July 18, 2011, available at http://bits.blogs.nytimes.com/2011/07/18/privacy-isnt-dead-just-ask-google/?pagemode=print.

24. United States v. Jones, 2012 U.S. LEXIS 1063 (U.S., Jan. 23, 2012).

25. People v. Weaver, 12 N.Y.3d 433, 441-442, 909 N.E.2d 1195, 1199 (2009).

26. *Jones*, supra at *39 (concurring opinion).

27. Id. at *52.

28. Id. at *46.

29. Id. at *50.

30. 18 U.S.C. §3123(a) (2011).

31. *Jones*, supra at *27 (concurring opinion).

CHAPTER SEVEN

The quotation from Justice Jackson in the epigraphs to this chapter is from Terminiello v. City of Chicago, 337 U.S. 1, 37 (1949) (Jackson, J., dissenting). The quotation from Justice O'Connor is from Hamdi v. Rumsfeld, 542 U.S. 507, 536 (2004) (plurality opinion of O'Connor, J.). The quotation from Justice Powell from United States v. United States District Court, 407 U.S. 297, 313–14 (1972).

    1. See Geoffrey R. Stone, *Perilous Times: Free Speech in Wartime* (New York: Norton, 2004).

    2. Boumediene v. Bush, 553 U.S. 723 (2008).

    3. See Stephen J. Schulhofer, *The Enemy Within* (New York: Century Foundation Press, 2002), 11.

    4. Id.

    5. U.S. Dept. of Justice, Office of Inspector General, *The September 11 Detainees: A Review of the Treatment of Aliens Held on Immigration Charges in Connection with the Investigation of the September 11 Attacks* (April 2003).

    6. U.S. Dept. of Justice, Office of Inspector General, *A Review of the FBI's Handling of the Brandon Mayfield Case* (March 2006), pp. 75, 259–64. See also Ashcroft v. al-Kidd, 131 S. Ct. 2074, 2089 (2011) (Ginsburg, J., concurring); Human Rights Watch and American Civil Liberties Union, *Witness to Abuse: Human Rights Abuses under the Material Witness Law since September 11* (2005).

    7. See Mayfield v. United States, 504 F. Supp.2d 1023 (D. Ore. 2007), vacated on other grounds, 599 F.3d 964 (9th Cir. 2010).

    8. See Stephen J. Schulhofer, *Rethinking the Patriot Act* (New York: Century Foundation Press, 2005), pp. 55–59.

    9. See id., p. 61.

    10. 31 U.S.C. § 5312 (2003); see Schulhofer, *Rethinking*, p. 62.

    11. U.S. Dept. of Justice, Office of Inspector General, *A Review of the FBI's Use of National Security Letters*, pp. 107, 109 (March 2008).

    12. See Pete Yost, "Rise in FBI Use of National Security Letters," *Washington Post*, May 9, 2011.

    13. Olmstead v. United States, 277 U.S. 438, 478 (1928) (dissenting opinion).

14. *The 9/11 Commission Report: Final Report of the National Commission on Terrorist Attacks upon the United States* (New York: Norton, n.d.), p. 394 (emphasis added).

15. United States v. United States District Court, 407 U.S. 297, 300 (1972).

16. 50 U.S.C. § 1801, et seq.

17. See In re Sealed Case, 310 F.3d 717 (Foreign Intelligence Ct. Rev. 2002).

18. See Schulhofer, *Rethinking*, 43–49.

19. P.L. 110–261, codified at 50 U.S.C. § 1801, et seq.

20. Richard A. Posner, *Not a Suicide Pact* (New York: Oxford University Press, 2006), pp. 9, 31–32.

21. *United States v. United States District Court*, supra at 315–17.

22. Stephen Holmes, "In Case of Emergency: Misunderstanding Trade-offs in the War on Terror," *California Law Review* 97 (2009): 301, 302.

23. Stephen J. Schulhofer, Tom R. Tyler, and Aziz Z. Huq, "American Policing at a Crossroads: Unsustainable Policies and the Procedural Justice Alternative," *Journal of Criminal Law and Criminology* 101 (2011): 335.

24. A 2007 National Intelligence Estimate identified the growing strength of al Qaeda in western Pakistan as the principal danger to the United States. National Intelligence Council, *National Intelligence Estimate: The Terrorist Threat to the US Homeland* (July 2007), p. 5. By 2010, the President's National Security Strategy gave heightened emphasis to "the threat…posed by individuals radicalized at home." As of mid-2010, of 202 people charged with serious terrorist crimes since September 11, 2001, more than half have been U.S. citizens, and over one-third of those have been American-born. See Karen J. Greenberg, "Homegrown: The Rise of American Jihad," *New Republic*, June 10, 2010, at 6–7; Jerome P. Bjelopera and Mark Randol, Congressional Res. Serv., No. R41416, *American Jihadist Terrorism: Combating a Complex Threat* (Dec. 7, 2010).

25. Schulhofer, *Rethinking*, p. 71.

26. Id.

27. Tom R. Tyler, Stephen J. Schulhofer, and Aziz Z. Huq, "Legitimacy and Deterrence Effects in Counterterrorism Policing: A Study of Muslim Americans," *Law and Society Review* 44 (2010): 365.

CHAPTER EIGHT

1. See James Gerstenzang, "Bush Presses Case for Spying," *Chicago Tribune*, Jan. 24, 2006 (quoting President George W. Bush as saying, in defense of the administration's regime of warrantless electronic surveillance, "We have ways to determine whether or not someone can be an al Qaeda affiliate or al Qaeda. And if they're making a phone call in the United States, it seems like to me we want to know why").

2. Leach v. Three of the King's Messengers, 19 Howell's State Trials 1001, 1027 (King's Bench 1765), discussed in chapter 2.

3. Brinegar v. United States, 338 U.S. 160, 180–81 (1949) (Jackson, J., dissenting).

Further Reading

. . .

Alschuler, Albert W. Racial Profiling and the Constitution. *University of Chicago Legal Forum* (2002): 163–269.

Cuddihy, William. *The Fourth Amendment: Origins and Original Meaning.* New York: Oxford University Press, 2009.

Davies, Thomas Y. Recovering the Original Fourth Amendment. *Michigan Law Review* 98 (1999): 547–667.

Harris, David A. *Profiles in Injustice.* New York: The New Press, 2002.

Holmes, Stephen. In Case of Emergency: Misunderstanding Tradeoffs in the War on Terror. *California Law Review* 97 (2009): 301–57.

Kamisar, Yale. In Defense of the Search and Seizure Exclusionary Rule. *Harvard Journal of Law and Public Policy* 26 (2003): 119–40.

Kerr, Orin S. The Case for the Third Party Doctrine. *Michigan Law Review* 107 (2009): 561–96.

Kerr, Orin S. The Fourth Amendment and New Technologies: Constitutional Myths and the Case for Caution. *Michigan Law Review* 102 (2004): 801–51.

Lasson, Nelson B. *The History and Development of the Fourth Amendment to the United States Constitution*. Baltimore, Md.: The Johns Hopkins Press, 1937.

Maclin, Tracey. Black and Blue Encounters? Some Preliminary Thoughts about Fourth Amendment Seizures: Should Race Matter? *Valparaiso University Law Review* 26 (1991): 243–70.

Murphy, Erin. The Case Against the Case for the Third-Party Doctrine. *Berkeley Technology Law Journal* 24 (2009): 1239–53.

Posner, Richard A. *Not a Suicide Pact*. New York: Oxford University Press, 2006.

Rule, James B. *Privacy in Peril*. New York: Oxford University Press, 2007.

Schulhofer, Stephen J. On the Fourth Amendment Rights of the Law-Abiding Public. *Supreme Court Review* (1989): 87–163.

Schulhofer, Stephen J. *Rethinking the Patriot Act*. New York: Century Foundation Press, 2005.

Schulhofer, Stephen J., Tom R. Tyler, and Aziz Huq. American Policing at a Crossroads: Unsustainable Policies and the Procedural Justice Alternative. *Journal of Criminal Law and Criminology* 101 (2011): 335–80.

Sklansky, David Alan. Is the Exclusionary Rule Obsolete? *Ohio State Journal of Criminal Law* 5 (2008): 567–84.

Smith, M. H. *The Writs of Assistance Case*. Berkeley: University of California Press, 1978.

Solove, Daniel J. *The Digital Person*. New York: New York University Press, 2004.

Solove, Daniel J. *Understanding Privacy*. Cambridge, Mass.: Harvard University Press, 2008.

Strandburg, Katherine J. Home, Home on the Web and Other Fourth Amendment Implications of Technosocial Change. *Maryland Law Review* 70 (2011): 614–80.

Warren, Samuel D., and Louis D. Brandeis. The Right to Privacy. *Harvard Law Review* 4 (1890): 193–220.

Index

. . .